The NeuroHorizons Primer

Empower Yourself to Empower the Child With Special Needs

Experiential Movement® as Science, Toolbox & Art Form

SYLVIA LEINER SHORDIKE
Founder of the NeuroHorizons® Experiential Learning Programs

with

KERSTIN BALDISCHWIELER
Founder of the NeuroScanBalance® Feinmotorik Training Programs

PUBLISHED BY NEUROHORIZONS RESOURCES

THE NEUROHORIZONS PRIMER

Copyright © 2020 by Sylvia Shordike. All rights reserved.

Cover photos copyright © 2008, 2019 by Sylvia Shordike.

First Print Edition: June 2020

ISBN: 978-1-7350830-1-8

Library of Congress Control Number: 2020909876

Published by NeuroHorizons Resources

info@NeuroHorizons.world

NeuroHorizons®, *Experiential Movement®*, and *A Child's Neural Map is Not the Territory®* are registered trademarks of Sylvia Shordike.

NeuroScanBalance® is a registered trademark of Kerstin Baldischwieler.

Feldenkrais® and *Feldenkrais Method®* are registered trademarks of Feldenkrais Guild Corporation California. *Awareness Through Movement®* and *Functional Integration®* are registered trademarks of Feldenkrais Guild of North America Corporation California.

Anat Baniel Method® and *NeuroMovement®* are registered trademarks of Movement Coordination Learning, Inc. DBA Anat Baniel Method Corporation.

To the remarkable children who
weather the challenges and drink in new learning,

their devoted parents and caregivers
who seek out and embrace new possibilities,

and the steadfast professionals who guide both
toward each new developmental horizon.

CONTENTS

WELCOME
From Sylvia & Kerstin

1
WHY MOVEMENT IS LIFE
Everyday Neural Plasticity

2
THE REMARKABLE REPERTOIRE
*Experiential Movement to
Embody, Envision, Elicit, Empower*

3
THE CHILD'S CURRENT NEURAL MAP
Is Not the Territory

4
EMBODIMENT IS THE MAIN EVENT
And It's Not a Spectator Sport

5
WALKING OUR TALK
The Best We Can Be

6
EMBRACING THE PROCESS
Not Selling a Product or Promises

7
THE EXPECTATIONS TRAP
Managing Anxiety and Ego

8
WHEN THE PROCESS SEEMS STUCK
Our World, Client's World

9
THE SELFLESSNESS OF SELF-CARE
Presence Requires Boundaries

10
EMBODIED PRACTICE AS ART FORM
Organized Improvisation

11
FOREST *AND* TREES
Into the Wild
With Our Relational Presence

A FINAL NOTE
Science, Toolbox & Art Form

Appendix A: *Daily Tips & Tools for Caregivers*
Appendix B: *The Feeling Child*
Appendix C: *About "Distance Learning"*
Glossary: *Key Terms & Concepts*

Dear Reader:

If you have not yet personally experienced our work for yourself or for your child, portions of this *Primer* may not at the moment make much sense to you. Our method of movement education is fundamentally *experiential* and *sensory* in nature — hence our highly personalized training and continuing education programs — and is not readily conveyed in words. While the Lesson Repertoire to which we refer throughout this *Primer* comprises many rather specific instructions regarding movement, it is not our purpose in the *Primer* to describe the "how-to" mechanics of our work. We instead consider some bigger-picture concepts about *who — and how — we are as practitioners* of Experiential Movement.

WELCOME
From Sylvia & Kerstin

This little *Primer* serves as a "welcome" for our new trainees, for the professionals taking our continuing education programs, and for all others who dedicate themselves to optimizing their support of Children With Special Needs. It is also the handbook we wish someone had written for us decades ago, as we first set out on our professional path as movement educators.

Whether we be parents, caregivers, or professionals, each of us in our own way commits to a journey with these great kids. The adventure can of course be challenging, yet also profoundly creative, transformative, and joyful. For our part, we authors want you to become as empowered as you can be, so that in turn you empower these children. Having now been movement practitioners, teachers, and trainers for (collectively) more than 50 years, we realized it was time to write down some key lessons we have learned about how to best support children facing diverse and complex challenges — while enhancing our own well-being along the way.

As is obvious from its small size, this *Primer* makes no attempt to cover the depth, breadth, or "how-to" detail of our movement education work with children. That's the role of our *NeuroHorizons*® training and continuing education programs. Here, we explain a little about why we have found our approach to this work to be so effective, and so personally and professionally rewarding. We focus on several overarching concepts, attitudes, and practices that reliably lead to the empowerment of both practitioner and client. Put another way, this *Primer* is about *who* — and *how* — *we are as practitioners*, not so much about the specifics of what we *do* with a particular client. We invite you to consider that, to the extent you integrate these principles into your work, many other details may fall into place as you evolve your skill and grow your clientele.

Over the years we have learned — from the many hundreds of kids and colleagues around the world we have been honored to support — not only which attitudes and approaches consistently lead to excellent client outcomes. We have also seen how one reliable and recurring fact of life tends to trip up parents and professionals alike:

> We often feel the urge,
> but can never successfully
> *"do it to"* or *"do it for"* the child.

Our *Primer* is based on a simple premise: As practitioners we are not joining some campaign to *fix* a child's developmental challenge or disability. Our aim is not to *manage* a "problem" with some convenient — yet likely superficial or temporary — band-aid or salve. Rather, we are *inviting* the child's brain and nervous system to discover and embrace new, empowering, and enduring ways to meet the world. With this gentle approach, children *create for themselves* something that wasn't there before, *on their own terms and timetable*. This is an organic, unforced *process* arising from *within* the child. As practitioners we help elicit and frame this *native exercise of neural plasticity,* but we cannot impose or control it.

While our premise is simple to state, it is not always so easy to apply in our daily work with the kids. This *Primer* walks you through a few key concepts that will help you:

- *Experience* for yourself *the gift of neural plasticity* and change;

- *Embody* what we call *Experiential Movement*® as an empowering framework for such neural plasticity and change, first for yourself and then for your young clients;

- *Evolve* your self-awareness, sensitivity, "differentiation", and "personal organization" in ways that optimize not only your own well-being, but also your spacious and attuned *relational presence* with each client;

- *Translate* your own embodied presence to *envision* and *transmit* meaningful *kinesthetic* and *sensory experiences* that *invite, elicit,* and *cultivate* each child's native, unique learning *process;* and

- *Prioritize your own self-care* and address unproductive expectations and attitudes — of both practitioner and caregiver — in order to reduce anxiety and stress, and to thrive personally and professionally.

In short, we want you to more fluently *move with* each child toward their optimal developmental trajectory, regardless of the challenges. We want you to *empower yourself to empower the child.*

Our professional success hinges on an appreciation that *a child's current neural map is not the territory;* on our humble and curious embrace of the *joint* "dance" of experiential learning; on our willingness to tolerate a largely unscripted adventure through *unchartered neural terrain* toward each new developmental horizon; and on our ability to anticipate, avoid, or address a number of common challenges and pitfalls along the way.

All this may seem like a lot to ask for. After all, most of us never learned these concepts or skills at home, or in school, or in our other careers. Yet, it can all be learned — and deepened — whether you are a trainee, a new practitioner, or already have a thriving professional practice. No matter our current level of experience, there is always a creative, novel way to enliven and elevate our skill and service. And we can do so while *enjoying more ease, grace,* and *pleasure* in our personal and professional life.

This *Primer* may be small, but some of its concepts are not. They invite unhurried reflection, and perhaps a personal recalibration or two. A number of real client vignettes in our last chapter are offered to help you imagine how you might bring all these attitudes and approaches together into your own work with children. Just as we encourage our trainees and continuing education colleagues to slow down and nourish a more relational, spacious connection with both self and clients, we recommend that you take your time feeling into these pages. May they help you crystallize your appreciation of our wonderful work, and further illuminate your path as an empowered and empowering movement practitioner.

Sylvia Leiner Shordike
Kerstin Baldischwieler
May 14, 2020

1
WHY MOVEMENT IS LIFE
Everyday Neural Plasticity

The late Dr. Moshe Feldenkrais famously said: *"Movement is life."* What does this mean?

If we are alive, we are constantly in motion, even those of us with challenging physical limitations or disabilities. The skeleton moves. Muscles and tendons move. Tissues move. Organs and glands move. Blood moves. Hormones move. Neurotransmitters move. Within and around every cell of our body countless components of life are in continuous motion. And, every part of the body is connected through movement to every other part. Most importantly for purposes of this *Primer*, the human brain learns and orients through movement. During waking hours the nervous system is largely occupied with the countless and unceasing movements noted above. That is, movement organizes our perceptions, interpretations, feelings, thoughts, intentions, and actions. Our very consciousness — and that includes new learning — relies on movement.

It follows that *attentive* and *intentional movement is a great way to communicate with the nervous system, and to re-organize and enhance our life.* Put another way, the *awareness* we bring to the character and quality of our movements — whether we be adult or child — will largely determine the character and quality of our *experience* of life. This foundational concept guides our work with Children With Special Needs. As practitioners, personal awareness of our own quality of movement underpins our ability to offer transformative learning opportunities to our young clients, who do not yet have such self-awareness. We will have more to say later about how this process unfolds.

> **Bringing awareness to our own movement — and to a child's movement — is a powerful way to communicate with the nervous system and open the door to an enhanced quality of life.**

Paradoxically, we often know good movement when we see it in others, but generally are unaware of it in ourselves. We love to watch elite athletes and how they move, or a fluid dancer, or musician, or martial artist. Conversely, bring to mind an occasion when you glimpsed a stranger in the distance, and immediately identified that person as "frail", or "elderly", or "disabled". You most likely came to this conclusion instinctively, based on the person's posture, gait, balance, and use of head and limbs — that is to say, their quality of movement.

Yet, how aware are we at any given moment of the intention, quality, and outcome of our *own* movements? Ask yourself: "Right now am I aware of my breathing, posture, pulse, or muscle tone? How conscious am I of the motion I just made? As I sit, stand, or walk, am I at ease and balanced, or tense and straining? Do I feel integrated and whole and "present" in my own skin, or scattered or stressed? Am I living so much in my head, intellect, anxiety, or daydreams that I cannot readily answer these questions? Have I wondered lately whether my life is moving too fast? Might I benefit from slowing down and becoming more attuned to my inner landscape? What keeps me from doing so?"

Genuine embodiment can be challenging even for "healthy" adults (we movement professionals included). Now consider a child with developmental challenges. Many disorders, diseases, and delays experienced by children interrupt the normal "conversation" that takes place between a child's nervous system and the "outside" world. Lack of full and free movement is a common element of these challenges. As just a few examples: A child who suffered a perinatal stroke or has cerebral palsy may have severely spastic limbs, preventing fluid, integrated, or fully bilateral movement; or, a genetic disorder may result in a constricting skeletal or brain malformation; or, a traumatic birth experience may lead to a rigid or listless baby who cannot readily tap into the usual developmental movement experiences; or, a kid with ADHD acting on impulse may not yet have the resources to attend to his inner landscape and develop a sense of self-agency and control; or, a child on the autism spectrum might be easily overwhelmed by any activity outside a very narrow internal comfort zone. Any such limitations present a dilemma for the child: Normal development is a progression of learning through movement and sensation, and the child may be missing key experiences that the nervous system needs in order to take a next developmental step.

This is why we often find a Child With Special Needs at an impasse: He may be missing the prior experiences required for optimal learning. For example, if the infant does not make use of the relationships among head, spine, and pelvis, he cannot learn to transition between positions, such as by flexing and rolling. It will be difficult to functionally use the arms and hands to push. There will not be a pliable spine and mobile pelvis. Hence, the self-generated skills of sitting, standing, and walking will not be possible to master. In other words, if certain interim movement experiences go missing owing to developmental deficits, the child cannot easily sequence his way to the next step. There is no "fast forward" button we can press to simply skip over those experiential gaps to arrive at the desired "developmental milestone".

> *For the child, learning is a process that evolves, movement by movement, sensation by sensation. When prerequisite experiences are missing, optimal learning may be stymied.*

Fortunately, it is nearly always possible to use gentle movement and sensory experiences to begin a new conversation with the nervous system of a child. Regardless of the diagnosis or developmental challenge, most young brains are available and ready for such kinesthetic learning and a transformational journey. As practitioners, our starting point necessarily is the developmental impasse at which we find the child. That is, we meet each child where she *is*, not where we or a parent might think she is "supposed to be". Through the *Experiential Movement Lessons* we discuss a little later, the child's brain and nervous system eventually receive and assemble the information, experiences, and conditions required for new abilities and mastery. With the practitioner's insight, skill, and patience, these Lessons can mitigate or even remedy many of the developmental gaps and deficits caused by various conditions and traumas. The child can then natively *do*, and *be*, in ways not possible before.

> **We enter a conversation with the child's nervous system via gentle, directed sensory and kinesthetic experiences. The child's brain can then receive and assemble what is necessary to fill developmental gaps and explore new skills.**

Key to our understanding is that the body is a collection of *neural networks*. Each such network is a grouping of nerve cells that "fire and wire together" and are responsible for some aspect of how we experience, perceive, interpret, react to, and move in our environment. Repetition strengthens existing neural networks: The connections we use the most become stronger and endure — whether for good or ill. We humans universally define and view ourselves through these habituated, and largely unconscious, neural patterns. Some such patterns are useful, such as never forgetting how to write our name, ride a bicycle, tie our shoe, or brew our morning coffee. But neural networks also account for why even our acknowledged "bad habits" can be so hard to break — and we all have more than a few of these. The engrained patterns have become our "default" mode, our "autopilot", the path of neural least resistance.

Conversely, think of a time you felt satisfaction, even excitement, learning or experiencing something (or someone) new. This is the pleasure of new neural networks forming — the process of *neural plasticity*. New networks can be formed even in our adult and aging brains, and eventually displace the primacy of older patterns and habits that no longer serve. Yet, this does not always happen on its own; we often must *intend* to make it so, or at least welcome rather than resist new information and experiences when they knock on the doors of our awareness. As practitioners, both our personal and professional work is about opening those doors — for ourselves and for our clients.

We are all born with this capacity for neural plasticity, through which our nerve cells change the way they are shaped and relate to one another in existing or newly-created neural networks. Both structurally and functionally, new neural communications and patterns arise in response to environmental factors, social interactions, and new information and stimuli (such as the Lessons we explore for ourselves, and offer our clients). It is such "newness" in our life, not the familiar "been there, done that", that best activates our learning process.

And, as we have noted, movement is an everyday yet potent way to elicit these changes. This is why we engage our clients in *novel* and *varied* movement, while emphasizing the "experiential" of Experiential Movement. As noted, children are particularly receptive and adaptive when it comes to creating new neural networks. Hence the effectiveness of our intentional movement work, especially when offered in a manner that helps the child to feel safe, affirmed, and loved.

> *Experiential Movement activates and cultivates neural plasticity in a child's receptive brain. With insight, skill, and patience we elicit and nurture this learning process, empowering the Special Needs Child to explore new horizons.*

This *learning process* relies, first and foremost, on our confident embodiment of these movement principles *for ourselves*. That is, we slow ourselves down and get friendly with our own attentive and unhurried process of forming new neural networks. We are then present enough to *envision* and *move with* a child in ways that evoke and empower his own experiential learning. Together, practitioner and child create a "safe container" and attend to novel and varied movements, unveil new neural horizons, and embark on new developmental trajectories. We will talk much more about this *joint* adventure throughout the *Primer*.

Our leveraging of neural plasticity is greatly facilitated when we foster a *heart connection* with the client. Neuroscience continues to tease out the complex interplay between the head (nervous system) and the heart (cardiovascular system). The heart hosts its own neural networks, and independently senses, processes information, makes decisions, and initiates considerable communication with the brain. The heart not only responds to stimuli, but generates its own neurotransmitters and hormones. Through its rhythmic activity the heart helps determine the quality of our emotional experience, our perceptions, and our cognitive function and problem-solving. In other words, both head and heart are necessary for new learning. We return later to the twofold importance of our heartfelt interactions with our clients: They power the practitioner's discerning and intuitive vision for the learning process, as well as the child's ease and willingness to embrace the "dance" into new neural territory.

We will say it in different ways over the following pages: The child is receptive to new learning, no matter the challenge. As embodied and relational movement practitioners, we identify creative and meaningful ways to gently dance with the child's native resources. This is what allows both client and practitioner to move beyond the existing map toward new neural networks. This profound appreciation — *that a child's current neural map is not the territory* — is key to our successful support of the child through movement.

2

THE CHILD'S CURRENT NEURAL MAP
Is Not the Territory

We use the name *NeuroHorizons* to describe our experiential training and continuing education programs for parents, caregivers, and professionals. This is because we like to think in terms of *developmental horizons* as they relate to the new learning and *neural plasticity* we can activate in children through directed attention and intentional movement experiences.

The horizon is something that we can see, even if only in our mind's eye. It's a place we want to get to, though we still have a journey ahead of us. And we never quite know what is going to happen on our journey through that as-yet unexplored territory, or what we will find when we get there. Indeed, along the way that territory and the horizon are always shifting, as we become more aware, and see further, and then explore to the next new horizon, and so on.

This is exactly the continuing adventure we engage in as embodied practitioners of Experiential Movement. As we invite a child's new awareness, experiences, and learning through movement, we are journeying *with* the child through previously undiscovered neural terrain. Both of us are exercising our neural plasticity, and building new neural networks. We eventually find ourselves in places we have never been before. And, we are actually expanding the territory of possibilities as we go.

Now, we all would like to think we have a good map of our reality. But for any of you who have taken a hiking trip through an unfamiliar wilderness, this next part may sound familiar. Before the trip, we get the best, most detailed map we can find — for example a topographical map that shows precise elevations, contours, landmarks, water features, trails, and many other details.

Yet even for the best map readers, a funny thing happens when we actually get to the area that the map describes: We find things that we did not anticipate. There may be unexpected landscape features or obstacles — such as a small yet impassable cliff, or dense underbrush, or deep mud, or a rockslide — that the map did not reveal. There may be better alternative routes through the terrain that were not obvious from the map. The camping areas we were counting on may turn out to be too wet, too rocky, or too exposed. We may stumble across surprising flora and fauna, for better or worse. And, when we are fortunate, we may be rewarded with magnificent scenery that no map could ever convey.

In other words, until we arrive at the actual location, a map can only give us so much information. The reality is much, much more than the map. Indeed, once we arrive our actual experience tends to supplant the map altogether. And this is why people have said over the years that "the map is not the territory". This metaphor reminds us to fully live and grow from the actual experience, not to blindly rely on someone else's summarized description of it. Working as we do with so many clients, we know that the same metaphor applies to our wonderfully unpredictable journey with the kids. This is why we amended the old saying to read: "A child's neural map is not the territory".

> *Paradoxically, we begin our journey with each child relying on the constrained neural map that the child presents.*
>
> *Yet, we always hold in our awareness that this map is merely an introduction to a much richer territory yet to be unveiled.*

Neuroscientists have documented how the "brain maps" responsible for our various human functions can be modified and even created anew, based on changing circumstances and learning. One example might be a person who loses function in part of the body or brain due to an injury or a stroke; he nevertheless may be able to develop a new neural "map" that at least partially compensates for this loss and allows similar functions to take place despite the loss. In short, the brain is quite able (especially when we apply our intention and attention) to change its structure and function.

In our work with Children With Special Needs, such neural plasticity is an essential element of the learning process. For example, a child may come to us with habituated spasticity, uncontrolled movements, lack of self-awareness, or various reflexive and unproductive behaviors. All of this comprises the child's existing neural map. It is this current map that typically consumes a caregiver's attention — we all tend to focus on what is demanding our attention right now — and may distract us from imagining, exploring, and experiencing a far wider range of possibilities.

Our distinction as practitioners is that we are in effect inviting each child to gently "dance" with us in a *joint* adventure of discovery *beyond* the current map. *Together* we unhurriedly and spaciously explore the contours of the child's neural terrain — and in fact grow and expand that territory — through intentional movement. We accomplish this through our skilled selection of Lesson elements, and our emphasis on *variation* and *differentiation*. That is, through diverse and often unfamiliar movements we invite our clients to experience themselves and the world around them in new ways. We help kids uncover and tease out their unique and often unexpected pathways toward the formation of new neural maps. These may at least partially repair or compensate for a child's deficits, shifting him into the best possible developmental trajectory according to his situation.

In short, we practitioners help activate the client's *native* learning process. Our "dance" elicits new neural networks, which begin to "fire and wire" together and over time displace the old patterns. The child who had not been able to do this on his own, owing to developmental challenges, can now receive and assemble critical new information. He gets curious, experiences new sensations and options, and enjoys a pleasurable sense of safety, skill, self-agency and confidence. This all unfolds at his own pace, which is sometimes rapid, and sometimes incremental. Like the seasoned map-reader mentioned earlier, we don't presume to know ahead of time just how the journey will unfold, or what will be revealed. We follow the child's lead and timing, until he is ready to explore toward the next neural frontier, and so on.

The key takeaway is this: All of us — children, parents, and practitioners — have habituated patterns in our body and brain that are reflected in how we move, or don't move, or think, or make and act out our life choices. These are like the paper topographic maps we mentioned, but instead are embedded in our neurobiology. And we often don't recognize that we are reflexively following such patterns, because we have become so accustomed to them. We may not even consider that we have options.

Yet, with intention and attention we eventually learn that these habituated maps do not reflect the full range, diversity, and promise of our neural territory and potential. Whether adult or child, we can continually re-shape and expand our neural maps, growing and shifting our realities throughout our lives and despite our limitations. Better yet, we can accomplish all that through our everyday, intentional movement. And, as empowered practitioners we are in the singular position to invite our young clients to experience this empowering learning process for themselves.

> **A child's habituated neural map
> is our starting point, but never the ending point.**
>
> **Our greatest gift to our clients is our ability to
> creatively and fluidly "dance" with them
> through an expanding neural territory
> toward each new developmental horizon.**

Our journey with each child through this neural territory is fueled and framed by the *Experiential Movement Lessons* we offer. Our success hinges on how well we have embodied the *Lesson Repertoire* for ourselves.

3
THE REMARKABLE REPERTOIRE
Experiential Movement to Embody, Envision, Elicit, Empower

For more than fifty (collective) years we authors have worked with untold hundreds of children facing diverse and often profound challenges (such as cerebral palsy, stroke, body and brain injuries, scoliosis and kyphosis, ADHD, autism spectrum, and numerous genetic and congenital disorders). We have seen some truly remarkable changes in these great kids, often far beyond what other professional helpers had expected. What is this all about?

Our practice of *Experiential Movement®* is inspired by the groundbreaking repertoire of hundreds of *Awareness Through Movement® Lessons* and *Functional Integration® Lessons* created by the late Dr. Moshe Feldenkrais, D.Sc. (1904-1984). He was the polymath physicist, mechanical engineer, judo expert, and educator who originated the *Feldenkrais Method®* using principles of physics, biomechanics, and an empirical understanding of learning and human development. Dr. Feldenkrais was passionate about guiding individuals to better "organize" themselves and *"move with minimum effort and maximum efficiency, not through muscular strength, but through increased consciousness of how movement works."* His lessons addressed the movement of virtually every part of the body, and their many inter-relationships. Through numerous books and trainings he emphasized the whole being — body and brain, sensations and emotions, imagination and intention, learning and change, dignity and freedom.

> **"The lessons are designed to improve ability, that is, to expand the boundaries of the possible: to turn the impossible into the possible, the difficult into the easy, and the easy into the pleasant."**
>
> M. Feldenkrais, Awareness Through Movement, p.54
> (Harper & Row 1972, 1977)

Dr. Feldenkrais had described as early as 1949 the role of the nervous system in determining the quality of the individual's learning and life experience. Notably, he presented the essential concept of neural re-patterning decades before the phenomenon was widely known or accepted, even among scientists.

> **Long before the term "brain plasticity" entered our vernacular, Dr. Feldenkrais observed that *"rigidity, whether physical or mental . . . is contrary to the laws of life."* Yet, habitual unproductive behaviors tend to endure *"unless the nervous paths producing the undesirable pattern . . . are undone and reshuffled into a better configuration."***
>
> M. Feldenkrais, Body and Mature Behavior, pp. 13, 40
> (International Universities Press 1949, 1988).

By 1981 he was explicit: "*You can, at any time of your life, re-wire yourself....*" * As importantly, Dr. Feldenkrais was perhaps the first to offer a practical, accessible method of movement education for leveraging this inborn capacity for re-wiring — the specific *Awareness Through Movement* lessons noted above. The genius of his discoveries is that, through our attention to gentle variations in movement, we can all experience this *learning process* for ourselves, and elicit such neural plasticity in our clients as well.

---

* Dr. Feldenkrais described how the "neural substance organizes itself" so as to "order" our experience of the world.

"My way of looking at the mind and body involves a subtle method of 'rewiring' the structures of the entire human being to be functionally well integrated, which means being able to do what the individual wants. Each individual has the choice to wire himself in a special way." Indeed, "You can, at any time of your life, re-wire yourself...."

M. Feldenkrais, The Elusive Obvious, pp. 25-27, 117
(North Atlantic Books 1981, 2019)

While this "subtle method of rewiring" ourselves through attentive movement can be transformative for anyone, Children With Special Needs often enjoy particularly welcome outcomes. Dr. Feldenkrais was the first to show practitioners how to work in this manner with Special Needs Children, through gentle movement lessons. His legacy endures: Today, the various movement education training programs of our genre, however they may brand themselves, rely on his pioneering insights as the foundation of their work. At *NeuroHorizons* we refer to this body of knowledge as the *Lesson Repertoire*. We offer clients and colleagues our particular interpretation of these insights through what we call *Experiential Movement Lessons*, with an emphasis on "experiential".

The "Mechanics"

The "mechanics" of our method can be simply stated: Experiential Movement Lessons are gentle and directed *movement sequences* that help the nervous system become more aware of the whole self, including the many inter-relationships among body parts and functions. This attention activates neural plasticity, and results in new skills, options, and ease with the tasks of daily living. We empower ourselves to unveil and choose among meaningful possibilities that best suit *our own* body and unique life circumstances, rather than someone else's. We move and feel better, and think and act with more clarity, freedom, and potency. When we can do this for ourselves, we are then able to envision and elicit such experiences for our clients.

The Attitudes and Intentions

Yet, all this can only come to pass when we embrace a set of interdependent *attitudes* and *intentions*. Let's take an initial, brief look at some key considerations. We will talk more about these throughout the *Primer*.

- ⊙ *Slowing Down Into Awareness, Presence, and Learning*

    When we are not in a hurry, we can create the *spaciousness* necessary to notice the finer details of our reality. We become *present* to ourselves, and more fully activate and experience our senses. With this *awareness* and *attention* we can then explore our own movements. Through our unhurried exploration of the Repertoire we are likely to discover more optimal ways to move through life. We experiment with *variation* and *differentiation,* and thereupon expand our choices and better "organize" ourselves.

**"To know fast and slow in oneself is extraordinary".
Whether for ourselves or our clients, to learn means to "go slower, so that you can organize yourself to your action by making a fundamental change in yourself. If you go fast, you don't allow it. Learning must be made so slow, that in everybody's makeup, activity can be organized."**

M. Feldenkrais, The Master Moves, pp. 54, 194 (Meta Publications 1984)

As we slow ourselves down, we get out of our own way. It then also becomes easier to sustain a *relational presence* with our clients. This allows us to more readily *envision, invite,* and *elicit* the child's *native learning process,* rather than *impose our own* preconceptions or agendas. We do this moment-by-moment — in "real time" during client Lessons — based on continuous feedback loops among child, practitioner, and parents.

Research confirms that the human nervous system does not typically respond well to being "rushed", "stressed", or "forced" into unfamiliar "learning" situations. Nor are repetition and imitation, by themselves, great ways to learn new skills. For example, if a child cannot yet by herself roll or crawl, push, sit up, be on all fours, or stand or walk, simply imposing these positions or repetitive exercises is not likely to optimize her sensitivity, differentiation, or learning.

Hence, in our work we serve as a *source of evocative movement experiences.* We *invite* each child to *create for themselves* something that wasn't there before. This is possible owing to our attuned and relational attitude. In our unhurried and gentle Lessons together, the child's nervous system experiences a "safe container" for new learning.

- *Variation, Differentiation, Organization*

We all tend to move habitually, which does not necessarily mean optimally. Typically we don't give much thought to our movements, much less consider the possibility that there may be a different way (or many different ways) of achieving the same result, and with considerably more ease and elegance. As for our young clients, many never had a full opportunity to explore such options, owing to their developmental challenges.

As practitioners, our unhurried presence allows us to explore novel and varied movements, which in turn lead to enhanced "differentiation". We use this term to mean *recognizing* differences, *creating* differences, and freely *choosing* and *transitioning* among those differences. Through our exploration of the Repertoire we become aware of how we use particular parts of our body, how those parts interrelate with each other, and how each movement ultimately involves our entire body and sense of self. From such awareness comes new possibilities.

"[T]he truly important learning is to be able to do the thing you already know in another way. The more ways you have to do the things you know, the freer is your choice. And the freer your choice, the more you're a human being."
To have such a genuine "free choice",
the "difference must be significant".
M. Feldenkrais, The Master Moves, pp. 20, 119

To become "differentiated" in some aspect of ourselves means that we are capable of freely choosing among a variety of ways of going about the same movement. The result is an ease and function that we did not have before — an enhanced personal "integration" or "organization". This freedom initially requires an investment of energy, in the form of our *intention* and *attention*. For the practitioner, this means an ongoing exploration of the Repertoire to enhance our personal and professional vitality. For the child, it means experiencing the Lessons the practitioner offers.

The practitioner's invitations *elicit* the child's native learning process, through her own experience of novel and varied movements tailored to her circumstances. This may involve elemental yet crucial movements, such as using the arms and hands to push or lean; becoming aware of different body parts and how they are connected; crawling, rolling, or sitting; or self-transitioning to all fours, standing, or walking. There may be greater spatial awareness and orientation, enhanced mobility and coordination, or improved gross or fine motor skills.

Whatever their specific path, kids begin filling gaps in experience, as mentioned earlier. The child gains self-awareness and options. This leads to a sense of agency, self-confidence, and power. New neural networks begin "firing and wiring" together, displacing habituated patterns that no longer serve. Kids shift into the best possible developmental trajectory, according to their particular circumstances. We offer several client vignettes in Chapter 11 illustrating some of the myriad ways this process can unfold.

Consider that our exploration of *differentiation* is not a purely mechanical or intellectual exercise. It calls upon *all* of our resources — for ourselves and for the children we serve.

Differentiation is a gestalt:
"It's imagination. It's appreciation. It is feeling
both in space and in ourself. It is listening, thinking, feeling,
appreciating both internally and externally what's happening.
How the body moves in space."
M. Feldenkrais, Amherst Training Comments (1980)

⊙ *Sensitivity, Imagination, Vision*

On the one hand, Dr. Feldenkrais described a "subtle method of rewiring" ourselves. On the other hand, he noted that the differences we cultivate "must be significant". It may at first seem paradoxical, yet to experience such *significant* differentiation we actually have to get very *subtle* with ourselves, and with our clients. Rather than "trying hard" to move in new ways, we *reduce* our effort, strain, and striving. This is what allows us to become more sensitive to small differences in how our body moves and feels. With such subtlety of attention, awareness, and movement, we can meaningfully explore options that may better serve us, or our client.

"More delicate and improved control of movement is possible only through the increase of sensitivity, through a greater ability to sense differences."
M. Feldenkrais, Awareness Through Movement, p.59

> "Sensitivity increases only when you reduce the stimulus, that means you reduce the effort."
>
> And, to "increase your sensitivity you must increase your organization.... The movement feels easy and light.... Disorganization feels difficult, disagreeable."
>
> M. Feldenkrais, The Master Moves, pp. 25, 75

Through our own unhurried and subtle experience of the Repertoire, we practitioners become more aware, sensitive, differentiated, and empowered. We then begin to understand on a profound level the new, empowering choices that may be possible for a child with developmental challenges. Thus, it is our *own* enhanced "organization" that allows us to *imagine* and *envision* a path toward an enhanced organization for a child beyond her developmental impasse — that is, the particular kinds of movement experiences and variations that may best bring her attention to the parts of herself that are out of awareness, or habitually held in limiting patterns.

Through the "dance" of the Lessons we translate and transmit our own organization in service to enhancing the child's organization.

⊙ *Our Humble and Curious Surrender Into the Dance*

As noted, we don't *impose* but rather *invite* the child into learning *opportunities*. We continually send out these *invitations* to the client's *native* capacity for neural plasticity. We like to say we are asking each client to "dance", and then we are *dancing together* — fluidly, spaciously, and creatively — toward new neural networks and developmental horizons.

Note that we are not using this dance to *"do it to"* or *"do it for"* the child; that would deny the child her own experience and pace of self-empowered learning. Indeed, any effort by us to control the process likely will delay or derail the client's native experiences needed to carry her to the next developmental horizon.

> **Rather than "impose", we continually "invite"
> the child to "dance" with us into learning
> opportunities and new neural networks.
> We are each following the other's lead.**

As this is a *native* learning process, it necessarily unfolds on each child's unique terms and time schedule, not ours. In this sense, the Child With Special Needs is in charge of her own "developmental stages" and "milestones". We *let go* of any rigid or particularized preconceptions, expectations, or goals of our own regarding how the specifics of each client's development will unfold, or when. This attitude calls on us practitioners to put aside both our insecurities and grandiosity. We must be willing and able to tolerate a *largely unscripted adventure through the unknown*. We fluidly adapt to the child's learning needs in each new moment, rather than try to squeeze her into some preconceived or generic therapeutic formula, protocol, or routine.

"It is important to realize that people are biologically different from one another . . . .

> *[T]here are individual modes of action, movement, feeling, and sensing which make each individual a unique case . . . he must be treated to help him in his uniqueness."*
>
> M. Feldenkrais, The Elusive Obvious, p.72

It follows that there is no single "right way" to give a Lesson to a child, but rather a number of *empowering* ways to elicit a particular client's native learning process in each unfolding moment. To achieve its promise, our work requires of the practitioner a sensitivity and humble curiosity to keep asking in a Lesson: "I wonder . . ." We continually tune in to what kind of learning this child might best make use of *now*, and *now*, and *now*. We envision a meaningful path forward and ways to connect. Then we improvise, mix, match, and test myriad elements of the expansive Repertoire. All this happens in "real time" as each Lesson unfolds. In this "safe container" for learning, head and heart of practitioner and client work together as a powerful and empowering team supporting the "dance" into new neural territory.

- *Awareness as Empowerment*

Dr. Feldenkrais liked to emphasize the nature of our personal dignity and potency. To the extent we live our lives doing what we are told, or what we think is expected of us, we are not deeply feeling and knowing ourselves and our options. We will not be whole, or free. Hence his lifelong emphasis on enhancing awareness through movement.

> *"[W]hen the coachman is wide awake and holds the reins the horses will pull the carriage and bring every passenger to his proper destination.*

> *In those moments when awareness succeeds in being at one with feeling, senses, movement, and thought, the carriage will speed along on the right road. Then man can make discoveries, invent, create, innovate, and 'know.' He grasps that his small world and the great world around are but one and that in this unity he is no longer alone."*
>
> M. Feldenkrais, Awareness Through Movement, p.54

In a nutshell, our debt of gratitude to Moshe Feldenkrais is for his empowering concept of using movement to foster new learning and neural networks — through growing our own unhurried and subtle awareness, sensitivity, variation, and differentiation. With a humble, curious, and spacious relational presence, we in effect translate and transmit our personal organization for the benefit of Children With Special Needs. We imagine how best to bring the Repertoire into our "dance" with each child, empowering them as they discover, explore, and expand their own neural landscape. We thus *embody*, *envision*, *elicit*, and *empower*.

Neither the "mechanics" nor "attitudes" of this approach are what we typically learn in our families, schools, or jobs. You already know that in our hectic and often virtualized world, a genuinely embodied, relational presence is a rare and precious human resource. It requires care and feeding even within families and among loved ones. Yet, such presence is the singular, distinguishing feature of our professional training and service to the kids. It is our *marvelous métier*, and at *NeuroHorizons* we champion it.

4

EMBODIMENT IS THE MAIN EVENT

And It's Not a Spectator Sport

As noted earlier, Experiential Movement Lessons work because we are all born with the capacity for neural plasticity. Our exploration of intentional, varied, and differentiated movement creates new learning and neural networks, and eventually displaces old patterns. And, our personal *embodiment* of the Repertoire, along with our *relational presence*, are how we transmit this learning so as to empower the kids. This largely defines the movement education services we offer as practitioners, and sets our work apart. But what exactly do we mean by "embodied, relational presence"?

Recall that our work is not about "doing it *to*" or "doing it *for*" the child. Instead, our role is to serve as an ongoing *source* of experiential movement that evokes and cultivates each client's unique and *native* learning process. We are supporting each child to *create for themselves* something that wasn't there before. As we suggested in the last chapter, this requires more than mere mechanics or technical skill.

The brilliance and beauty of the Lesson Repertoire is this: When we slow down and deeply experience and embody the elements, the gestalt, and the outcomes of a Lesson for ourselves, *change happens*. We are more *aware* of and better *organized* in our movement, moment by moment. We are quicker to notice and turn off our "autopilot", and reconsider reflexive habits that may no longer serve. We thereby become more alert, at ease, efficient, vital, and effective as we go about our life.

The more familiar we get with our *own* learning process of differentiation and organization through movement, the better we can tune in to each child's unique version of that process. That is to say, our *personal* organization is what enables us to develop a relational, intuitive, nimble, and fluid connection with our clients. Indeed, our genre of movement education only exists because Dr. Feldenkrais himself engaged in years of self-exploration and experimentation, and was therefore able to show others how to enter this embodied learning process *for themselves*.

> **When we experience how change happens within ourselves, it is much easier to envision how change can happen for our clients.**

Put another way: Serving as a movement practitioner *is not a spectator sport*. If I don't personally drop deeply into a Lesson, I don't experience my body or inner landscape in new ways. I don't discover variation and differentiation, or create new neural networks or new learning for myself. I don't change. And if I don't change, I won't develop a first-hand appreciation of the transformative services I offer, or confidence in my work. My ability to support my clients on their own journey of change will be limited.

> "[U]nless you learn how **you** change
> when you get the right organization for you,
> you're obviously unable to detect that change
> in anybody else."
>
> M. Feldenkrais, Amherst Training Comments (1981)

Thus, in our work with the kids we all do well to monitor and occasionally ask ourselves: Do I remain intimately engaged with Experiential Movement for myself, embracing *my own* ongoing learning and organization? Am I *translating* and *transmitting* the qualities of my own embodiment in tailored ways that are meaningful and empowering for this particular child? If I am not feeling able at the moment to identify, elicit, and cultivate the learning needed by a client, what might I do to re-calibrate and re-start the dance *with* the child?

> **By cultivating our own self-awareness,**
> **new neural networks, and embodied self-confidence,**
> **we can powerfully support the kids to grow theirs.**
>
> **So we first embody for ourselves**
> **that which we want to offer others.**

Personal organization is not solely about *how* we move. It also includes our "inner landscape" and "feeling self". Habitual patterns and "held" musculature — and associated impairment of function and vitality — may reflect our reactions to difficult (and often repressed or long-forgotten) life experiences. Perhaps we were injured or hospitalized early in life. We might have been partially immobilized with a brace, or cast, or medication. We may have learned to "defend" against stressful family or environmental circumstances by holding our breath, clenching jaw and facial muscles, tightening our chest and shoulder girdle, and repressing feelings. And years later, after the original "reason" for our constrained movement is long gone, we often don't even recognize that we remain on "autopilot", unwittingly limiting ourselves as we reflexively persist in these old patterns or coping strategies.

As we explore Experiential Movement, sometimes such "old material" surfaces. Novel movements entail novel sensations, lead to new connections, and can evoke unexpected feelings and epiphanies. These may range from the initially unfamiliar or disconcerting, to pleasurable, to liberating. That is, the Repertoire leads us into a more intimate and integrated relationship with the *whole* self. This is no less true for our young clients. A number of the vignettes described in Chapter 11 illustrate this aspect of our work. We say more in *Appendix B* about how the child's physical *and* emotional vitality go hand-in-hand, and how the practitioner can help the child integrate unexpected feelings into the learning process and new neural networks.

The more attuned, respectful, and kind we become toward our own "feeling self", the deeper can be our empathic bond with clients. And, the stronger our heartfelt connections with the kids, the safer they will feel and the more fruitful will be our time together. You might recognize a similar dynamic from your experience in personal or workplace relationships — when we exercise some empathy and compassion, and "upgrade" our own attitudes and behaviors, those around us tend to reciprocate. Such mutually reinforcing "mirroring" at the level of our neural networks has been confirmed by neuroscience.

For the practitioner, our connection directly supports our capacity for a discerning and intuitive vision for the learning process. For the child, the connection creates a "safe container" for new learning and makes the Lesson personally engaging; he is more likely to embrace our moment-by-moment invitations to "dance" into new neural territory. Not to mention that we both have considerably more fun together!

For all these reasons, in our movement work we routinely (albeit generally unconsciously) make good use of the complex interplay between the brain (nervous system) and the heart (cardiovascular system). We noted earlier that the heart hosts its own neural networks, and independently senses, processes information, makes decisions, and initiates considerable communication with the brain. That is, both the practitioner's heart and the client's heart directly support the learning process. By cultivating our heartfelt relational presence with a child, we invite a reciprocal heart connection *from* the child — even when he is quite young or has severe deficits.

> **Head and heart of both practitioner and client work together as a powerful and empowering team supporting the dance into new neural territory.**

You have gathered by now that the child's remarkable learning process does not simply result from the "mechanics" of "giving" him some movement lessons. We necessarily adopt some key *attitudes* and *intentions* that bring our work to life, as noted in Chapter 3. We honor and integrate *feelings* and *emotions* that surface during a Lesson. We nourish the *teamwork of head and heart*. By necessity we *modulate* our own emotional affect and the details of our "relationality" according to the temperament and needs of each child. In addition, the many possible Lessons we could choose to offer each can be layered with *variations*. Every child requires a tailored and skillful combination of Lesson elements, in different sequences, at different times, and with an approach that speaks to his unique circumstances in each new moment.

Thus, using the Lesson Repertoire with a client is never a linear exercise. Simply memorizing the "steps" of a Lesson, or going through movement sequences by rote, will be of limited value for the child. We will talk more about how, with experience, our curious, relational, and adaptive attitude becomes entirely natural and fluid — and an art form.

> **The power of Experiential Movement
> lies not in the mechanics of our "techniques" or
> "giving lessons", but in the attitude and quality of our
> self-aware, curious, and spacious relational presence.
> It is our own embodiment that allows us
> to envision and elicit the child's
> native and empowering learning process.**

We now have the broad strokes of how our "embodied, relational presence" plays out during an Experiential Movement Lesson. We are connected both to ourself and to the client — now, and now, and now. This attuned sensitivity is multi-layered, comprising our physical, feeling, cognitive, and intuitive presence. Our connection empowers us to effectively identify what the child may be experiencing (or *not* experiencing), such that we can *envision* possibilities for offering new information and evoking powerful new learning. We then can *translate* and *transmit* the qualities of our own embodiment of the Repertoire in tailored ways that are meaningful and empowering for this particular child. The neural mirroring and *mutuality* of our connection more fully engage the client in the dance. There is a continuous interplay of *feedback loops in "real time"* between child and practitioner, using *all* of our many senses.

> (*Note*: By its very nature, this *relational* — and therefore safe and empowering — learning process arises from our consistent and sustained *in-person* interactions with the child. In *Appendix C* we address some limitations of offering our services via "distance learning", such as by video conferencing).

In short, it is our prioritization of a fluid and multi-faceted *"relationality"* that makes possible client outcomes far beyond what techniques alone can offer. We sometimes say that this distinctive quality of *embodied presence* with the client — moment by unfolding moment — is our *marvelous métier*, in all senses of that word: It is at once our profession and calling card; our personal aptitude and expertise; and the outstanding quality that sets apart our service to the kids. If you enjoy comic book metaphors, you could also call such *relational presence* our collective "professional superpower", given the remarkable shifts the kids usually make over the course of our Lessons together.

> In our work there is no place for arrogance or conceit. We nonetheless honor our genuinely distinctive method and the potent, transformative learning process we help elicit in our clients.

> *Our quality of multi-faceted relational presence is our personal and professional métier – or, if you prefer the metaphor, our collective "professional superpower".*

All this self-awareness and personal organization may sound like a tall order, but it is quite do-able. Remember that most professions require a lot of practice, patience, and perseverance in order to develop competence and confidence. The good news is that *our* "marvelous métier" does not require years of academic "book learning", rote memorization, or examinations. Nor does our metaphorical collective "professional superpower" involve supernatural gifts or require divine intervention. We are in control of our progress through deepening into our *experience* of the Repertoire – and of ourselves – one Lesson at a time. Plus, we heartily agree with Dr. Feldenkrais that our *"hours of practicing awareness in movement or action remain the most absorbing and interesting time in our lives."* This is because *"[t]he feeling of being alive relates to the awareness of growing to be oneself."* (*The Elusive Obvious*, p. 96).

Naturally, our habits of embodied, relational presence grow over time, as we diligently practice our craft and take advantage of continuing education opportunities and professional supervision. As we evolve our own personal organization, we also evolve our service to the children. We become living and breathing models and resources for both our young clients and their caregivers. We are walking our talk.

5
WALKING OUR TALK
The Best We Can Be

    The Lesson Repertoire is a deep and wide treasure trove of practical, effective resources for practitioners and clients. No matter how many times the two of us authors explore a particular Lesson (and this is many times!) we always experience new variations and insights that enhance our own well-being, and by extension that of our clients. We relish all the *"Aha! moments"* that the Repertoire unveils for our personal life, and then translating those to support a child's own learning. And, these insights can come from deepening into even a single Lesson; we don't have to wait to "master" the entire Repertoire to be of great service to the children.

    From long experience we know that when *we gift ourselves the time and space* to deepen into the Repertoire, one Lesson at a time, our resulting *personal* mastery is what allows us to be masterful with our clients. And, the kids quickly recognize and respond to our embodied and relational confidence and competence.

    In other words, mechanics and techniques are great, but are not mastery. Our own evolving organization is. That is our short answer to students and colleagues who ask: *"How can I be the best practitioner I can be?"*

> *Our ever-deepening embodiment is the key to becoming and remaining the best practitioner we can be. This continual self-organization is how we thrive — personally and professionally.*

This answer is not as obvious as one might think. Occasionally we hear students or even practitioners grumble that a particular Lesson is "too long", or "too boring", or "too difficult", or "not relevant." Others may believe that because they have "done" a particular Lesson, or watched a video presentation, they now "know" a certain movement or technique and have all they need. Or, we might learn of some new and exciting piece of scientific research about movement and neural plasticity, which further illuminates and "validates" our movement education work. We then conclude that the method has now "evolved", or that by understanding this new information we have somehow become a better practitioner.

The human mind is expert at rationalizing that "knowing" something new and useful is an end in itself. But in our profession, if we have not *embodied* and *organized ourself* around that learning, we have not wired new neural networks, and we remain pretty much where we started. Our clients do not receive any tangible benefit from our mere intellectual "knowing." As Dr. Feldenkrais pointedly noted, *"intellect is no substitute for vitality." (The Elusive Obvious* p.69).

Put another way, all our wonderful *ideas* about the work are not the work itself. Nor are those ideas "re-inventing" movement education, or even "evolving" Dr. Feldenkrais' original method as such. Rather, our distinctive service to our clients lies in how we continually and fluidly "re-invent" and "evolve" *ourselves* through increasing self-awareness, personal organization, and relational presence with our clients.

> **Longtime Master Trainer Mia Segal, Dr. Feldenkrais' first teaching assistant and associate, says it this way:**
>
> *"It is not about 'evolving the method'. It's about evolving myself."*

So, we certainly want to learn and take full advantage of the many tools and techniques of our trade. We also love to learn about all the new discoveries of neuroscience that do, in fact, help explain why our work can be so powerful. But to be clear: If we have not embodied the relevant Lesson elements for ourselves, or if we treat them as an intellectual exercise, or apply them *to* a child by rote, we likely will be missing the forest for the trees — we won't grasp the bigger picture or envision our way into each child's optimal, native learning process. We will be dancing alone, with our clients passively looking on. Both they and we will be missing the full potential of what our method offers.

So let's get practical: Just how do we go about *embodying* the Lesson Repertoire, and getting better *organized* ourselves? How do we *envision* our way into the child's learning process? How do we creatively *translate* and *transmit* our embodiment in service to each client's needs? In short, how do we best support the kids to create for themselves something that wasn't there before?

First and foremost is this simple and non-negotiable professional obligation: Our own *regular experience* of the

Lesson Repertoire. As with an athlete or musician, consistent practice is essential to our own personal vitality and professional effectiveness. In our case, this means re-visiting and deepening into the many Lessons, one at a time and over time. We learn to add variations, mix, match, and explore. We get creative and have some fun with it all!

Indeed, this mindful practice, improvisation, and continual self-organization enliven our awareness and presence. These in turn allow us to be ever more attuned to, and present with, our diverse clientele and their myriad and changing needs. We can then more naturally envision meaningful ways to dance with the Lesson elements, and thus creatively support each new client on his or her own unique journey of empowerment.

> *It is our own ever-growing embodiment that allows us to imagine, attract, and creatively support a diverse clientele with myriad challenges and needs.*
>
> *Through our own relational presence, each unique child gains the experience of creating something that was not there before.*

Exploring an Experiential Movement Lesson doesn't require complicated logistics, and need not take a huge amount of time. Naturally, the more time you spend the more you will evolve your own neural networks and organization. But even when our day is full, just 10 to 20 minutes of a Lesson — whether on the floor, in a chair, on the table, or even standing — can still provide great benefits. And don't worry that you haven't experienced or embodied the entire (and extensive) Repertoire: Every little bit carries you forward, and you are already of service to your clients!

Also remember that it is not a problem if you have physical limitations that make it challenging to fully experience *all* elements of every Lesson. Keep sinking into the elements that you *can* do, improvise work-arounds, or simply activate your imagination and visualization. You will be dancing in the learning process and on your way to new neural networks.

> **There is no substitute for our regular, personal exploration of the Lesson Repertoire, even if only for minutes a day.**

How to choose from the expansive Repertoire the "best" Lessons to practice? Consider that you probably already know instinctively when you could benefit from a "tune up" by revisiting (or learning) a particular set of movements. You may be motivated by acute or chronic deficits, injuries, stiffness, or aches and pains. Or, a particular client situation may focus your awareness on the client's readiness for certain movements, and you realize you need to review and refresh your own experience. Or, you may simply want the *pleasure* of the movement, and the resulting fluidity.

It's always helpful to refer back to the relevant lessons as presented in your own training, which most likely derive from the original teachings of Dr. Feldenkrais. For current practitioners, video or audio lessons presented by *embodied* teachers can be very useful. And of course, we encourage our colleagues to take personalized continuing education seminars that focus on the *experience* of movement and *embodiment* of the Repertoire, to increase the potency of their work with the kids.

(*Note*: We generally do *not* recommend distance video learning for *trainees*. When orienting ourselves to this approach, we all need sustained in-person and personalized attention and guidance to activate and guide our own neural plasticity through movement. This is how we "get" what it means to embody the work, and how we grow our *subtlety* and *presence* with ourselves and with our clients. Ours is a deeply *relational* and *sensory* craft that cannot be learned remotely).

How do we best review and integrate these Lesson materials? As we watch, listen, or read, *we let go of our intellect*. With a *Beginner's Mind* (meaning empty, open, receptive, compassionate) we sink into each movement, without either pretense or self-judgment. We don't expect or aim for any particular outcome. We keep moving, and allow our *sensations* and *feelings* to flow freely, making adjustments as we go. We focus our awareness on the *experience* itself, *not* on some mental analysis of that experience — there will be plenty of time *after* the Lesson to reflect intellectually on any new awareness that has been unveiled.

> "[I]t's your feeling and experience of yourself that is more important than the explanation."
>
> M. Feldenkrais, Amherst Training Comments (1981)

Importantly, we do not stress, strain, or strive regarding the Lessons. Exerting oneself toward a goal is not the same as awareness or learning, and we approach the Repertoire accordingly — with a gentle, welcoming embrace of new neural connections. By simply experiencing our movement in each moment, we allow the learning, differentiation, and organization to become a part of our daily life, and then our dance with clients.

And this is our approach whether we have already experienced the Lesson many times over, or are exploring a less practiced or entirely new set of movements. We keep deepening into the Lesson until the *"Aha! moment"* that we mentioned earlier arrives. That is to say, our system has already started making new neural connections, and we can actually feel the sensation of new learning — which may be subtle, pleasurable, exciting, or invigorating.

> **Give your intellect a rest.**
>
> **Cultivate a Beginner's Mind.**
>
> **Surrender into the experience of each Lesson without mental analysis, expectation, or self-judgment.**
>
> **Savor the "Aha! moments" and pleasures as you welcome new neural networks.**

Now that we are embodying the Repertoire to become the best practitioner that we can be (no matter our current experience or skill level), we are ready to engage in the learning *process* with our young clients.

6
EMBRACING THE PROCESS
Not Selling a Product or Promises

Becoming a movement practitioner is exciting and profoundly rewarding. Even after more than 25 years each of professional practice, we both wake up every day looking forward to our work with the kids and their caregivers. We feel blessed to have a career that provides this kind of personal and professional fulfillment. Naturally, as with any compelling adventure, there will be unexpected bumps and detours along the way. We can minimize the distractions and disruptions by embracing our work with clients as a learning *process* rather than as a *destination*.

New practitioners typically face twin challenges: First, they may feel a bit overwhelmed by all the rich information from their trainings. Understandably, they really want to "do it right", and may experience some "performance anxiety". Second, their new clients are themselves often anxious and full of expectations. It is therefore not surprising that a new practitioner may worry about getting the "right" outcome for the client, overemphasize Lesson mechanics and checklists at the expense of a more embodied, relational presence, and thereby "miss the forest for the trees" in the client session. This is a good time to pause, breathe, and remember what our work is really about.

No matter our current level of experience or skill, our value to our young clients is that we are a *source* of experiential movement, awareness, and learning. We are offering a *process*, not a *product* or some specific or promised *outcome*. When we leave our own preconceptions, expectations, and agendas at the door, the process can unfold on its own rich terms, usually in ways we could never fully imagine. By tolerating a large degree of *humility*, *uncertainty*, and *surrender to the unknown*, we then can freely and fluidly "dance" and help elicit each child's native, optimal, and unpredictable path of neural plasticity.

This *learning process* — and our ability to creatively envision and dance *with* the children in a relational, *joint* adventure toward new neural networks — is in fact what sets our method apart from many therapeutic modalities. This process is why our clients often experience more change with us, compared to other approaches they may have tried. It is why clients come to us in the first place, and keep coming over time. It is why both of us authors and so many of our wonderful colleagues have added the Lesson Repertoire to prior bodywork, physical therapy, or medical expertise.

> **By continually focusing on our role as the source of a learning process rather than the purveyor of a product or promised outcomes, we won't miss the forest for the trees.**

We can illustrate the point with the example of the two of us. For decades we have worked with children presenting with most every kind of bodily or brain injury, birth trauma, or genetic challenge. So when a new client comes to us, by now we must know exactly what to do, right? To the contrary, we meet each new child without prejudgment, checklist, agenda, or itinerary. We allow ourselves to keep asking: "I wonder. . ." Which is to say, we get humble, let go of our preconceptions and expectations, and *get out of our own way*.

Now, please understand that this does *not* mean we don't know what we are doing! Nor do we lose sight of desirable outcomes. Rather, by starting with humble curiosity, we *create a spaciousness* in which we can get *relational* with the client. Using *all* of our many senses and intuitions, we are able to see and feel more clearly what the child is experiencing, or *not* experiencing. Through touch, sounds, communication, feeling, and of course many variations in movement, we begin to *envision* how we might best dance with each client into a powerful learning process. Our sustained "relationality" generates *feedback loops in "real time"* among practitioner, child, and caregiver. Like teasing out a thread from a tangled ball of string, we slowly but surely find a way into the child's unique developmental trajectory, moment-by-unfolding-moment.

> We cultivate humility, curiosity, and the continual question: "I wonder . . ."
> This spaciousness allows for "real time" feedback loops, and our vision for how best to dance with each child into a meaningful learning process.

Even after we have found our way into the child's learning process, we still do not predict how it will unfold, or on what time schedule. And we certainly do not try to force or control the process, which would of course defeat our purpose of allowing the child her *own* experience of self-agency, self-discovery, and native learning. We know that remarkable changes can sometimes come remarkably quickly, yet we also accept that progress can be slow and incremental, and include setbacks and regressions. And at times we may invite a caregiver to consider other resources they may need at the moment. Whether fast, slow, or postponed, we continually remind ourselves that *progress is a process.*

> **A seeming paradox is key to our success:**
> **By relinquishing our need for some particularized outcome, we optimize client outcomes —**
> **through eliciting and nourishing**
> **each child's native learning as it unfolds**
> **on its own rich terms.**

There is another great reason to fully embrace our work as a *process:* It helps inoculate us from both our insecurities and our arrogance. Yes, our work is empowering for a child. But that is very different than imagining that we are personally *responsible* to "fix" or "manage" this child, or conversely that we are a hero or miracle worker when wonderful shifts come. Rather, we envision and help frame the *circumstances* that allow the child to experience a native learning process, and to *create for herself* a reality that did not exist before. By getting out of our own way and embracing this largely unpredictable process, we won't so easily get discouraged, stressed, or burned out when progress seems slow. Nor will we get grandiose when outcomes are good.

In short, "letting go" — into the acceptance that client *progress is a largely unscripted and unforeseeable process* — is a profound support to our work, our clients, and our own health. This is especially so when stressed or impatient parents come with their own high hopes and expectations. How best to respond when caregivers are anxiously "waiting" for us to "produce" desired changes or "milestones" for their child?

7

THE EXPECTATIONS TRAP
Managing Anxiety and Ego

A major reason the two of us became movement practitioners decades ago, and still love our work, is that we so often see excellent outcomes: Kids gain confidence and become empowered as they learn and shift their experience of the world; parents re-focus their energies in enlivening and productive ways; and we as practitioners feel useful and fulfilled. Yet, we would be remiss not to mention that, on the way to these wonderful results, we at times encounter some challenging expectations, attitudes, and egos — both ours and those of our clients.

Some of the parents and caregivers who bring us their children are understandably anxious or desperate for progress or solutions. They read about the effectiveness of our movement work, or watch videos purporting to describe amazing client success stories. Maybe they latched onto the glowing client testimonials we practitioners like to highlight in our websites. For any of these reasons, a client may have unrealistic expectations, and place demands on us practitioners.

For example, many practitioners have had the experience of a new client expecting to see quick results, or even a "miracle" of some kind. Some parents want you to predict whether, when, or how their child will progress toward some milestone, such as: "Will Jane be able to [focus], or [swallow], or [crawl], or [sit up], or [start walking], and how soon?" Others may be waiting for us to push that non-existent "fast forward" button to skip over the gaps in learning and simply arrive at the desired milestone. And we have even heard some caregivers say things like: "Well, I hear that Practitioner X does it this way or that way, and gets much better results much more quickly. Why can't you?"

We might turn such client questions and attitudes into harsh verdicts about our competence: "If I can't get quick results I must be a lousy practitioner, and certainly not as good as that other Practitioner X". Perhaps "I'm just not capable of working with this client."

Or, we can take a deep breath, and let go of any inner voice whispering words to the effect of: "I told you that you aren't good enough for this work". We come back to our embodied, curious, and nimble connection with the child, in each moment asking ourselves: "I wonder . . .?" We stay relational with the child, don't take onto ourselves the caregiver's anxieties, and keep surrendering into our joint dance through the unknown.

> **By continually embracing the reality that the child's progress is a largely unscripted and unforeseeable process, we "pause" any anxieties, nourish our relational presence, and sustain the richness and power of the "dance".**

Along the way, we gently educate parents and caregivers about our method and the learning *process*. We may gently point out how the adult's own understandable stress and anxiety invariably affect the child, and can drown out new learning. By "walking our talk" we provide a model of slowed-down, relational presence that supports not only our child client but the adults who love and care for her.

Such self-confidence comes from being honest with ourselves, no matter the progress (or lack of progress) we perceive with a particular child. Let's just admit that we love to see (and take credit for) great outcomes with our young clients. And we may doubt (or blame) ourselves when good results are not immediately apparent. It is best to face this double-edged sword right up front.

On the one hand, there's a natural human tendency to take full credit for the good outcome. In any profession there will be some practitioners and teachers who enjoy making it all about themselves — "*nobody else can do it like I can.*" It is easy to forget that the child who experiences big changes from movement lessons almost always has received significant support before they came to us: Parents and caregivers, various therapeutic modalities, and our fellow movement practitioners may all have played key roles. This prior support often laid the groundwork for our own good outcomes. So we do well to give due credit and thanks to those who brought the child so far already.

We may also forget that it is the *child* who is doing the learning, and making the hard changes. It is neither our role as practitioners to "fix" the child, nor in our power to work miracles. Rather, we *envision* and offer *opportunities* for a meaningful learning *process*, through which our clients *natively create for themselves* something that wasn't there before. Indeed, we do ourselves and our clients a real disservice if we fail to acknowledge this simple fact: The child's highly "plastic" brain and nervous system are far more clever and capable healers for that child than any of us practitioners could ever be!

So yes, we congratulate ourselves for identifying and offering empowering opportunities. We savor our personal organization and creative *vision* made possible by our continuing embodiment of the Repertoire. We celebrate our fluent *translation* and *transmission* of all that in service to the client's learning process. And then, we honor the child (and her supportive caregivers) for doing the real work of running with the process that we offer, thereby creating and embracing their new neural networks.

> **We honor those who have laid the groundwork.**
>
> **We honor ourselves for our presence and skill offering meaningful learning opportunities.**
>
> **We honor the child and their brilliant nervous system for doing the actual work of change.**

On the other hand, when progress is not obvious, or slow and incremental, it is easy to doubt ourselves. Our perfectionism and "Inner Critic" may rear their heads, pulling us toward self-denial, insecurity, and distraction. If we notice this happening, we pause, breathe, and press the "mute button" on those voices, as they will never produce any benefit for the kids (or for us). We come back to our embodied self. If such "grounding" does not come easily for us, there are many systems of breathing, mindfulness, and meditation that can be helpful in this regard. Better yet, we can gift ourselves a few minutes to unhurriedly explore and experience a Lesson, and thereby renew our sense of integration and wholeness.

Of course, a particular client challenge may well inspire us to re-visit or learn a relevant Lesson that we could be more familiar with. We may need to shift our own awareness and approach. It may be invaluable to seek professional supervision from a trusted and seasoned colleague. We will talk more about these possibilities later.

But all that is very different than imagining that we should be delivering quick results "on demand", or that we are a failure when progress is not plain for all to see. We stay focused on the "main event": No matter our current skill level, we are offering each child our embodied, relational presence in support of their learning *process*. This always is an important service, whether some hoped-for "outcome" arrives quickly, incrementally, or for the moment not at all.

> **Our embodied self-confidence leads to
> ease, humility, and gratitude for the "main event":
> The child's unpredictable yet clever and capable
> native learning process that
> unfolds on the child's timetable, not ours.**

As noted, part of our role is to educate caregivers about our method and process. Consider that a parent new to our work may be conditioned to expect that a practitioner *does* something *to* the child to *manage* or *fix* a problem (like certain therapy protocols, exercises, or mechanical aids), rather than *invite* the child into a *learning process*. Caregivers may not yet grasp that in most cases, even for a seasoned and masterful movement practitioner, progress is indeed a process. And that process is, at times, incremental. While most parents might admit that their own "bad habits" can be hard to change, they naturally hope that it can be different for their child. We therefore inform parents and caregivers about how new neural networks are formed, and old patterns eventually left behind; these are physiological realities, but ones that generally require consistency and time. And none of us can predict any child's precise trajectory and timing.

It also happens that we, as trained practitioners, may see subtle yet important changes in a child when their caregiver does not. Even parents are not always as attuned as we are to notice gradual progressions. So again, we can gently point out our own experiences and observations. We foster *reality-based optimism and enthusiasm* by highlighting the child's real shifts — in alertness, curiosity, tracking, movement, etc. — even when small and incremental. We remind caregivers that such small shifts are the necessary building blocks of larger change. We may offer tips for how to support and continue the progress at home. And as appropriate we can offer to consult or collaborate with the child's other helpers. We will talk more later about how to go about this caregiver education process, without getting enmeshed or stressed ourselves.

Now, a time may come when we have done all of this, yet our work with a child still has not produced apparent shifts, even over a significant period of Lessons. What then?

8
WHEN THE PROCESS SEEMS STUCK
Our World, Client's World

The two of us authors have worked with countless children over the years, and continue offering Experiential Movement Lessons to these great kids most every day. We are pleased to report that in virtually every case we are a valuable resource for our young clients as they learn, shift, and move forward. We have no end of stories about kids and parents leaving our offices with big smiles, relief, and excitement for all the new learning and progress. Yet, there comes a time for every practitioner when it seems our work with a particular child produces no visible shifts, even over a period of regular and consistent lessons. We may even see a setback or regression. What now?

First, we remind ourselves yet again that our role is to offer a *process*, not to provide quick fixes or miracles. Sometimes this means client changes can be slow and incremental, or forward and backward and forward again. In a rare case it may even mean that our work is not what the child needs most right now.

If we are getting anxious or impatient about a child's progress, the first question is to *ourself*: Might I have unrealistic objectives for this client, or be projecting my own expectations or demands? For example, am I starting where the child is *now*, not where I (or a parent) thinks he "should" be? Am I really engaged in a spacious, fluid, *joint* adventure *with* the child? Can I tolerate the uncertainties of dancing with him through unknown, as-yet undiscovered neural territory? Am I on some kind of "autopilot", stiffly trying to impose some technique or "recipe" based on my *preconception* about what should be happening (or what I should be "accomplishing"), and how fast? Am I trying to prove something to someone?

We also notice whether we are experiencing any "performance anxiety", perhaps because the child (or parent) is stressed and anxious themselves, or is expecting big results? Or maybe because the client has been referred by a colleague whom we don't want to disappoint? Or might we have an unwelcome "Inner Critic" questioning whether we are really capable of this work?

Depending on our answers to these questions, we may want to press the "pause button", take a long, deep breath, and go about re-calibrating ourselves. We slow down, and stop "trying" so hard. We tune in to and get gentle again with ourselves (and by extension with our client). We adjust to a more self-aware and positive attitude, with the help of any grounding or mindfulness technique (or Lesson) we care to use.

In short, we *let go* and *get out of our own way*. We are now re-connecting with the client from a more embodied, relational, and fluid attitude, *which the child will almost certainly feel and respond to*. We have re-calibrated and re-started the dance.

> *Our first inquiry is an "attitude" self-assessment, and if necessary re-calibration. We get out of our own way and send out a renewed, revitalized invitation to dance. The child will almost certainly notice and respond.*

Second, we will step back and review our vision and approach, as well as the client's needs. We might ask:

- Is this child receiving Lessons frequently and consistently enough given his circumstances? Have I been clear with myself and with the parent about the possible benefits of more, or differently paced, work? Conversely, is the child's system overwhelmed by too much stimulation?

- Am I able to envision this child's empowerment and a possible trajectory? If not, why not? If so, has my vision crossed a line into an expectation, agenda, or demand?

- Is the child curious and engaged with my Lessons, perceiving small differences and shifts? Or does he seem resistant, "checked out", or bored? How might I more effectively translate and transmit my own organization into varied, interesting, and potent opportunities that activate this child's learning and re-organization?

- Could I review the Repertoire and get myself better organized with regard to the particular Lesson elements that are relevant to this child in the moment? How might I improvise, and creatively mix and match different elements and variations of the Repertoire, in order to reach this child?

- Have I arrived at an impasse that calls for perspectives or supervision from a seasoned colleague?

The answers are not always obvious at first, but just asking these questions will often lead us forward to a next step.

> Our second inquiry is about the quality of
> our own organization, presence, and vision,
> our choice of Lesson elements,
> and how we translate all this into a
> meaningful learning process for the client.

Third, we notice what is happening to the child between Lessons. Are the parents and caregivers allowing and supporting the learning process to continue to unfold between visits? If the child is working with other helpers at the same time, are we communicating and collaborating in a way that optimizes client benefits? Is the child engaged in other activities, or using mechanical aids, in ways that support or hinder progress in our Lessons? Are there family, cultural, or religious factors at play, such as unhelpful judgments about disabilities or how to approach them? Might we offer useful "daily tips and tools" that could make a difference for parent and child? (see *Appendix A*)

Now, we are mindful about keeping our *professional boundaries*: How the client and family live their lives is *not* the practitioner's business, much less something we have any power to change. When we become aware of issues that may be affecting the child's progress, we can certainly offer gentle observations, suggestions, and referrals to useful resources. But we do so *without expecting* or *demanding* that the caregiver follow our lead.

We are also careful not to critique or contradict medical or other professional advice, even if we have strong contrary views. We add our own observations and suggestions to the mix, but remind ourselves that *only* the caregiver can decide what is best for the child, and *choose their own path forward.*

In some circumstances a client may simply not be a good "fit" for our work at this moment. For example, a child may be engaged simultaneously in multiple modalities, one or more of which may be inconsistent with the relational, evocative, and fluid learning process that our own method calls for. In such cases we may point out the dilemma and suggest the parent choose just one modality that they want to explore at this time, in order to best recognize and optimize the respective benefits of each approach. Or, severe chronic spasticity in a child may lead to the parents' consideration of surgery, which could then allow our work to be more effective. Or, parents may face distracting life circumstances that cannot sustain the shifts that happen for the child during or after the Lessons. Or, a parent's attitude may not be conducive to our learning process — such as exhibiting complete disinterest in what we are doing with their child. Sometimes we realize that we are "spinning our wheels" because "external" changes are called for; with care and compassion we will direct the caregiver's attention to those considerations, and to any appropriate resources.

Finally, we humbly accept that *we cannot be all things to all clients.* Occasionally, we realize that our experience and skill at the moment are not best suited to a particular child. For example, we might refer a client to a colleague who specializes in the unusual developmental challenge that this child experiences. We may choose not to work with a physically large or strong child who has a condition that involves loss of control and possible injury (to the practitioner) during a Lesson. Rarely, despite our best "bedside manner", a child (or parent) simply may not respond well to us or the process we offer, for reasons we will probably never know.

> Our third inquiry is about the client's world, circumstances, needs, and constraints. What external factors might be causing us to "spin our wheels", require a pause in our work, or call for a referral to other resources?

In summary, when the client relationship feels "stuck", or the client seems disengaged or bored, first breathe and tune in to yourself. Consider whether *you* are the relational and fluid dance partner your client needs at the moment; if not, slow down and let go of any preconceptions or agendas, and re-connect. Be honest about your own level of embodiment and organization, and whether you might want to review and deepen into a particular area of the Lesson Repertoire. Collaborate with colleagues. Seek out and enjoy professional supervision. Get creative and improvise. Notice what else is happening in the client's world. Gently offer suggestions and resources, without expectation or demand, and while keeping your professional boundaries. Learn to gracefully make referrals rather than continue to spin your wheels.

Making these self-assessments and client assessments is a key to prioritizing our *self-care*, which is an essential ingredient of our personal and professional success.

9
THE SELFLESSNESS OF SELF-CARE
Presence Requires Boundaries

For the two of us, the biggest joys of our work come from the wonderful kids, and from their amazing, devoted parents and caregivers. We are continually inspired and energized to give our best, with pleasure and dedication. Yet, at times we can find ourselves feeling stressed, and we then know it is time to pause and reflect on what is happening.

By definition, our profession can present us with stressful situations. Some of the great children we support may be enduring very tough challenges. A parent might be dealing with layers of heartbreak, anxiety, anger, blame, guilt, shame, or depression. Marriages, families, and finances can be strained. Defensive — and usually counterproductive — family coping strategies may constrain learning opportunities for the child.

Understandably, we practitioners *really* want to help, to shift reality, to make things better. After all, that's why we chose this profession in the first place. And we nearly always help the kids and their families make those shifts!

Yet, it can happen that we start losing ourselves in the drama or overwhelm around us. As noted earlier, our *marvelous métier* (or "professional superpower") of relational presence means we are highly receptive, empathic, and caring. We can be deeply affected by the misfortunes and hardships of our clients. It follows that we may find ourselves irritated by attitudes or choices within the family, or school system, or medical world that we believe are counterproductive to a child's progress. We might have our own strong professional (and personal) opinions about preferred next steps for the child, which may not be shared by an anxious parent who remains wedded to (in our view) unhelpful therapies or achieving typical "milestones" on some schedule. Or, right on cue, the occasional parent at their wits' end may see us as their last hope to finally get the "right" analysis and solutions to their problems, putting us on the spot (and feeding our natural desire to help).

> **Ironically, our marvelous métier
> (or "professional superpower") of relational presence,
> and our gifts of empathy, compassion, and caring,
> can make us susceptible to
> unhealthy enmeshment and stress.**

We have most likely crossed the line if we are no longer feeling *at ease* in a client relationship, or are feeling *responsible for,* or *directive* or *anxious about* an outcome. Such entanglement mutates our gift of "relational presence" into a kind of undifferentiated fusion with the client. In this enmeshment we lose our ability to serve as an embodied, objective, and skilled guide for the client.

For example, our creative *vision* for an empowering learning process may have morphed into an *expectation* or a subtle *demand* for change. This might take the form of an agenda — conscious or unconscious — to achieve certain outcomes, on some time schedule, so as to reduce everyone's stress and validate our usefulness (or justify our fee). We might notice ourselves insistently giving directives. For instance, we may make it our business to "prescribe" the client certain dietary or lifestyle changes, medical or mechanical interventions (or discontinuation), or even parent or family counseling. We may become so invested in our clients that we imagine we have the exclusive right to work with them, to the point of telling caregivers that we are the best or only practitioner for their needs; we then get angry or jealous or flattened when they exercise their choice and explore other options. You can imagine how such attitudes might become a recipe for resentment — both toward and from our client caregivers. Frustration and stress ensue. This is not a good way to support the kids, or to enhance our own health and well-being.

> **Self-care is selfless, and essential to support our clients. So we are mindful to discern the difference between offering our relational presence in service to a child's learning process, versus counter-productive and stress-inducing entanglements.**

We do well to keep in mind that the practitioner's value to the client arises from our:

- Embodied self-awareness and relational presence (*tuned in to, but not entangled with, client challenges and hardships*);
- Clear observations, creative insights, and steady yet fluid approach to the learning process (*not clouded by rigid agendas, expectations, or enmeshment with the client*); and

- Personal vitality and effective use of the Repertoire (*free of unnecessary and debilitating stress or conceit*).

In short, attempting to "manage" or "fix" client problems is *not* our role, in fact hobbles our effectiveness, and is of no lasting value to the client, or to us. The punchline is this: *Keeping clear personal and professional boundaries, and prioritizing our own self-care, are acts of selflessness.*

> *Our metaphorical "professional superpower" is our creative, fluid, vital, and relational presence. Without ongoing self-care and clear boundaries, we will quickly lose that power.*

Here are some things the two of us do to enhance our own boundaries and self-care. We don't pretend that we get all of this right all of the time, but we do keep these considerations front and center:

- No matter how full our schedule, we set aside time for regular exercise, rest, reflection, and nourishment. We aim for a full night's sleep. We do our best to take weekends and vacations for ourselves.

- We prioritize our self-awareness and self-organization, because these promote our own health and vitality, as well as serve our clients. So, every day that we can, we deepen into an Experiential Movement Lesson and our embodiment of the Repertoire, even if only for minutes at a time.

- We continually acknowledge and relax the double-edged sword of our insecurities and grandiosity. We focus on the learning *process*, and keep *letting go* of any agenda, or illusion that we should or could be a heroic "fixer" or miracle worker. We are grateful and enthusiastic for even incremental changes (which we point out to the caregivers). We give due credit to the child's other helpers who came before us, and who will come after.

- From this place of "letting go", we deeply listen to and grasp each client's story and circumstances, without merging or losing ourselves in it. Through our attuned and relational presence we envision how we might dance with this child. We improvise learning opportunities in each unfolding moment, without getting attached to any particular outcome or time schedule.

- We gently but firmly resist requests (or our own ego temptation) to analyze caregiver problems, or give them the "right" answers to their life questions. We do not diagnose or prescribe, or contradict medical advice. We of course add our own opinions to the mix of possibilities they are considering. But we do so without arrogance, disdain, demand, or expectation. We accept the caregiver's ultimate choices about lifestyle, therapies, and practitioners, even if we might prefer different choices.

- No matter how healthy our boundaries or positive our client outcomes, we seek out and make room in our schedule for continuing education courses, consults with seasoned colleagues, and professional supervision. These are essential investments in our personal embodiment and vitality, and hence our continuing professional success.

"Please take care of yourself. If you don't, nobody will."
M. Feldenkrais, Amherst Training Comments (1981)

Please note that our clear boundaries do not require that we leave our clients stranded without resources between Lessons. We mentioned earlier that one of our roles as practitioners is to point out even subtle shifts in the child. This fosters a reality-based optimism and enthusiasm in the caregivers. Such positive feelings are not merely for the benefit of the adults; these attitudes get modeled and transmitted to the child at home, and are invaluable for good outcomes. It follows that we will often want to share our ideas for how caregivers can nourish the child's continuing progress on a daily basis at home. Indeed, many parents actively seek our advice and support. How do we offer such "daily tips and tools" in ways that nourish the parents' enthusiasm, without enmeshment, expectation, or demand?

First, we acknowledge that we cannot "outsource" our expertise to a caregiver; any "daily tips and tools" we choose to offer are a support, not a substitute, for in-person Lessons. Second, we know that not all parents will have the time, temperament, or circumstances to implement what we might readily envision as practitioners. Third, we accept that even the most conscientious caregiver likely will have to be reminded multiple times of any suggestion we make; we are asking them to change their own habitual patterns, so we graciously respect their own learning curve (and pace of neural plasticity). We don't take it personally when such changes come slowly, or not at all.

With those cautions in mind, we practitioners can offer a variety of "daily tips and tools" to support the child's learning process at home, without counter-productive entanglement or enmeshment. We offer a few generic illustrations of such possibilities in *Appendix A*.

> When appropriate, and without demand or expectation, we may offer caregivers "daily tips and tools" to use between Lessons, tailored to their child's circumstances.

Now that we are dancing with our young clients from our embodied and relational presence, while maintaining our boundaries and prioritizing our self-care, we are ready to take our work to the next level. We are ready to become artists.

10

EMBODIED PRACTICE AS ART FORM

Organized Improvisation

Thus far we have briefly introduced both the science and the toolbox of our movement education work. To recap:

- Movement is an everyday, powerful way to communicate with the brain and nervous system. Our skillful use of the Lesson Repertoire can activate learning, engage our inborn capacity for neural plasticity, and create new neural networks that fill developmental gaps, mitigate deficits, or displace habitual patterns that no longer serve. Children in particular are receptive to this kind of learning through movement.

- We first embrace for ourselves a set of attitudes and intentions, such as slowing ourselves down into awareness, presence, and learning; exploring the Repertoire to experience variation, differentiation, and an enhanced personal organization; and refining our own sensitivity, imagination, and overall appreciation for the *gestalt* of how we move and learn.

- We then leverage our own evolving integration and embodiment of the Repertoire to identify and transmit tailored learning opportunities for our young clients. We offer gentle and directed *movement sequences* that help the child's nervous system become more aware of the whole self. This attention activates the child's neural plasticity, and results in new skills, options, and ease.

- We don't impose, but invite. We elicit the child's *native learning process*. We embrace a spacious, unscripted and largely unpredictable *dance* together through the unknown, as we follow each other's lead. We let go of any specific expectations or agendas. Our humble, curious, fluid, and heartfelt *relational presence* is our "*marvelous métier*" or "*professional superpower*", and biggest gift to our clients.

- Our gift to ourselves is our *self-care,* and personal and professional *boundaries*. These help shield us from both our anxieties and grandiosity, and allow us to avoid enmeshment, stress, and burnout. We thrive personally and professionally.

At least on our good days, we can pat ourselves on the back for bringing to our clients the better part of these attitudes and activities. We are truly "walking our talk". And, at these times we may notice that our work rises to a new level. We have entered the realm of *artistry*.

Ours is not an artistry in the sense of creating objects for their own sake (or for fame and fortune). Nor are we playing a theatrical role, fictional yet convincing. We are not creating or performing music, or writing a novel. Instead, we are artful in our *dance with the client's native learning process,* as we have been describing throughout this *Primer*.

We do share with other artists some similar aptitudes and objectives. Consider that most works of art are built of elementary components and principles, such as generic colors, textures, materials, lines, shapes, or perspective. When the artist taps into an inner vision and brings those "simple" elements together in creative, evocative, or beautiful ways, we consider it meaningful art. When the actor portrays elemental human strengths, flaws, and foibles in a compelling performance, the audience appreciates our shared humanity in a new way. The musician arranges and expresses a finite number of notes in infinite ways that speak to and evoke a deeper part of us, as does the writer with words. Those artists all embody their respective repertoires and then interpret and improvise with basic elements to achieve fresh, unexpected, and meaningful outcomes.

Thanks to our own relational presence, we practitioners of Experiential Movement tune into what each unique client is experiencing — or *not* experiencing — in every next moment, always asking: "I wonder . . . ." Like other artists, we tap into our personal organization and embodiment of our own Repertoire. We can then sense and envision what Lesson elements might be most evocative for each client's learning process. We select the most expressive colors, textures, perspectives, notes, chords, and phrasing (metaphorically speaking) from our wide palette, and translate and transmit those in ways that speak to the client and elicit new neural networks.

With time and experience, all this starts to come together naturally, and a wonderful thing happens: We intuitively, creatively, and spontaneously mix, match, and improvise particular movements, variations, and techniques with the children. We could call this kind of artistry "organized improvisation." Our impromptu yet skillfully tailored combination of "simple" Lesson elements optimizes each child's learning and developmental trajectory, with outcomes that can be unexpected, meaningful, and beautiful.

> **With experience we evolve the confidence and skill to engage in an artful "organized improvisation" with our clients, made possible by our personal embodiment of the Repertoire, and our fluid, heartfelt, relational presence and vision.**

To be clear, developing this level of artistry involves some experience with a diverse clientele, and a degree of mature self-confidence. We are willingly and humbly stepping into the unknown, and "stretching" ourselves beyond a literal or mechanical application of the Repertoire; we learn as we go about what works, and what is not so useful, for a particular child. This means that we have let go of our agendas, expectations, and any impulse to prove anything to anyone. We have pressed the "mute button" on our "Inner Critic", as well as any part of our ego that wants to "fix" the client or be the hero or heroine.

And yet, as we take each step into the unknown, we are protected by a wonderful safety net: Our embodied, relational presence keeps us from getting lost either in our anxieties or grandiosity. We are able to keep in view both where this child *is now*, and where she *might be* in each next moment with some tailored Lesson elements. Put another way, we are able to see both the forest *and* the trees as we dance with her toward each new neural network and developmental horizon.

To the untrained eye, this kind of artistry may appear "effortless". Pleasantly surprised parents often ask us: "How did you do that? It all seemed [so little], or [so easy], or [so smooth]". Wonderful client outcomes may at times seem almost "natural" or "inevitable", just like we might take for granted a celebrated painting, sculpture, or symphony, without fully grasping the mastery that made it possible. Still, mastery in our profession only results from our dedicated, patient, and passionate practice over time of the activities and attitudes we have been discussing throughout this *Primer*.

Ironically, it seems that the more capable we become, the more clients come to us presenting with complex challenges or variations that we have not seen before. At first we may feel unprepared, and "in over our head". So yes, we take a breath. We acknowledge our doubts or fears. We question and assess. We may re-visit (or learn) some relevant Lesson elements, or consult with a seasoned colleague or supervisor for perspectives and reality checks. But in the end it is our embodied, relational presence that deepens our connection with each new client, elevates our skill and service, and calls forth our inner artist. We then envision and tease out creative, unexpected, and often beautiful ways to support the client's learning process.

There is one final, critical secret to your personal and professional success as you bring your artistry into the client relationship: *Smile and create some fun!*

**Throughout his final Amherst Training,
Dr. Feldenkrais repeatedly reminded his students:**

*"To be helpful to yourself and others,
would you please stop being serious."*

"Seriousness won't improve anything except tire you."

> *"Seriousness betrays our insecurity and anxiety, when we are least capable of learning."*
>
> *"If you are so serious the learning will never be profitable. You'll never use it if it needs so much attention. It's useless for life."*
>
> *"So make it fun. Smile a little!"*
>
> M. Feldenkrais, Amherst Training Comments (1980-81)

To summarize: Breathe. Slow down. Let go. Connect. Be curious. Stop being so serious. Smile. Allow your intuitive inner artist to visualize and improvise from the Repertoire and your embodied, fluid, spacious relational presence. Enjoy dancing with your client through all the uncertainty and unknown territory, toward each new neural horizon. And savor the new vistas as they emerge from the mists.

11

FOREST *AND* TREES
Into the Wild With Our Relational Presence

As we have seen, Experiential Movement can be viewed as science, toolbox, and art form. We *embody, envision, elicit,* and *empower*. What remains to consider is how all this comes together while working with a particular client. When facing the complexities of a child with many layers of challenge and potential, what is it like to keep in view both the forest *and* all the trees?

Each of the following vignettes condenses into one (very partial) snapshot in time the experience of a child we have been privileged to support (we have changed names and some identifying details for client privacy). While it is necessarily a small sampling, we have aimed for a cross-section of circumstances, to help you notice some commonalities and synergies: The practitioners' humble yet nimble relational presence, curiosity, and vision; their creative and varied use of the Lesson Repertoire; and their choices about how to elicit and dance with the innate neural plasticity of diverse children.

You will note that some of the client shifts we describe arrived incrementally over a period of many Lessons. Others came rapidly. Our purpose is *not* to focus on the outcomes as such, or the timing. Nor do we attempt to describe all the movement variations and differentiation we introduced in these Lessons. Rather, these brief accounts illustrate key elements of the child's *native learning process*, as elicited by the practitioners' *attitudes* and *intentions* (as described throughout this *Primer*). Consider whether, without these, each child's experience might have been rather different.

In short, these are all illustrations of how the *empowered practitioner* can *empower the child*. We invite you to use these vignettes to imagine how *you* might bring an even more embodied and fluid relational presence into the dance of neural plasticity with your own young clients — moment by unfolding moment.

We have rather arbitrarily organized these vignettes as follows:

NO BETTER TIME THAN NOW
- Boldness on Behalf of a Newborn (Joshua, Age 14 days)

STARTING WHERE YOU ARE
- Using the "Here" to Get to "There" (James, Age 4)
- Taking it One Step At a Time (Joann, Age 7)
- Getting Unstuck and the Power of Collaboration (Jane, Age 2)

SEEING BEYOND THE OBVIOUS
- Changing the World With a Single Finger (Julio, Age 9)
- Don't Judge the Book By Its Cover (Josephine, Age 3½)

SLOWING IT ALL DOWN
- Unveiling the Inner Landscape (Jess, Age 2)

- The Power of Doing Nothing (Jennifer, Age 4)
- The Power of a Parent's "Yes" To Slowing Down (Johnny, Age 3½)
- Saying "No" To the Parent Who Won't Slow Down (Jill, Age 12)

RELATIONAL PRESENCE IN REAL TIME
- The Leisurely Unfolding Moment (Jackie, Age 15 months)
- Whispering to the Whole Child (Jojo, Age 10 months)

ORGANIZED IMPROVISATION
- Curling Into Connection (Jeremy, Age 11)
- The Power of Joy (Jack, Age 12)

NO BETTER TIME THAN NOW

Boldness on Behalf of the Newborn
Joshua: Age 14 days *(Sylvia)*

We are sometimes asked whether it might be "too early" for a small child to experience or benefit from our work. Our short answer is generally: *There's no better time than now.* The longer answer: *It depends* — on the nature of the developmental challenge, and weighing the investment in immediate Lesson intensives against the possibility that the child's lost learning opportunities and engrained habits may be considerably harder (and more expensive) to address later.

Consider the example of Joshua, who was born via a vacuum-assisted (suction) emergency delivery, with poor vital signs. Newborns often have a reflexive reaction to the intense mechanical pull of a suction birth, leading to muscular contraction. Joshua had such contractions in his neck and head regions, and the birth was further complicated by an underlying genetic disorder. He was left without the usual, automatic gag reflex, and no ability to suck or swallow. Joshua immediately required a feeding tube, and the pediatrician advised the parents it could take him up to 18 months to learn how to feed from a bottle. The parents were not happy with this prospect, and promptly consulted me.

Embodied, Relational Presence: I first met Joshua at 14 days old. He did not move much, and tired easily. It was clear to see, and using touch I confirmed, that his body was almost entirely low-tone, that is to say "floppy" or "limp". The exceptions were his rigid head, neck, and sternum: Joshua's face, jaw, and mouth were all tightly clenched. This was a severe developmental impasse, as the head, mouth, and tongue provide the infant's first connections with the world (through feeding and vocalizations). Sucking is an automatic reflexive ability, and is how we all begin discovering the world – and growing. Yet Joshua lacked this basic reflex, and would not progress well without it.

As I gently explored this held musculature, I noticed my own sensations and imagery: I felt like I was inspecting a fresh clam whose shell was sealed shut as tight as it could be (clams also have "siphons" to the outside world, somewhat like Joshua's feeding tube). My vision for Joshua was already forming: If this shell could be coaxed open — if Joshua could release his facial and jaw muscles, open his mouth, and use his lips and tongue — we would all be rewarded with the proverbial pearl hidden inside, namely a more optimal developmental trajectory for Joshua. But how does one go about offering Experiential Movement to a newborn facing such challenges?

I knew from my own adult exploration of the Repertoire that differentiation of the face, jaw, lip, and tongue muscles through movement makes a huge difference in both function and self-awareness. I was able to envision the same for Joshua, while of course "downscaling" my approach to match his tiny body. Softly and unhurriedly I began using movement and sensory experiences to introduce Joshua to an experience of his face, eyes, lips, and mouth. I used just the tip of my little finger, and of course my voice, to caress and invite. I alternated my attention between movement experiences involving his face, and then neck, sternum, and shoulder girdle. I followed the "feedback loops" and surrendered into the joint "dance" with this beautiful boy.

Outcomes: At the end of our first visit, Joshua pursed his lips ever so slightly, and I knew that his native learning process was activated. At our second visit his jaw began to release, and I was able to introduce him to his tongue. By the third Lesson he opened his mouth, pushed out his tongue, made sucking motions, and actually swallowed. At the fourth Lesson I was stunned to see the rapid change in Joshua's facial expressions and overall movement of the head and body; he was acting more and more like a "normal" baby. He began experimenting with breast feeding.

After just four Lessons over the course of a week, Joshua was well on his way toward much brighter developmental horizons. The rather surprised pediatrician confirmed Joshua's unexpected yet welcome gag reflex and ability to swallow. Needless to say, the parents were thrilled.

Takeaways: Joshua's parents deserve full credit for their quick action. They might well have waited for him to learn to suck and swallow on his own. We cannot know when or whether those reflexes would have come, given Joshua's multiple deficits and likely habituation to the feeding tube. Regardless, the parents' decision to act early was rewarded almost immediately; Joshua is now empowered with a very different developmental trajectory than others had anticipated.

Joshua's story illustrates many of the concepts we have talked about in this *Primer*. At only two weeks of age and despite severe deficits, Joshua's inborn capacity for neural plasticity was fully available for new learning. And he was a quick learner: Over just a few hours of gentle Lessons, Joshua could make a different use of his musculature, open his mouth, use his tongue, and gain the key reflexes missing at birth. He defied medical predictions and "schedules".

This was not an "intellectual" learning, but a native development of his nervous system. I could not have controlled this process even had I wanted to; his system knew exactly what to do, and did so in its own way and on its own schedule. What did I contribute? I stayed *present* with myself and my own sensations and imagination, which enhanced my spacious, *relational presence* with Joshua. I provided the *opportunity* for new learning that he was unable to generate on his own. My *own* adult experience and embodiment of the Repertoire allowed me to envision an empowering process for Joshua, and to *elicit* that process in our joint "dance" together. I did all this *slowly* and gently, giving him plenty of time to experience the variations and new sensations — and in just a few days the differentiation and new neural networks he needed to move beyond his developmental impasse. This combination of attitudes and experiential learning through movement is what we mean by *embody, envision, elicit,* and *empower*.

STARTING WHERE YOU ARE

Using the "Here" to Get to "There"
James: Age 4 *(Sylvia)*

Diagnosis: Genetic disorder resulting at birth in a severe kyphosis (extreme forward rounding of the spine) and scoliosis (sideways curvature of spine). Associated connective tissue disorders.

Deficits: James had virtually no movement in his spine, yet a kind of "floppy" weakness in his limbs. This resulted in an inability to use his skeleton to become and stay upright, and generalized instability. A wandering eye contributed to a lack of self-orientation. It was hard for James to be on the belly as he could not lift his head due to the kyphosis. He could not lean on his hands or push himself up through his arms. His lack of sequential learning meant he was missing the information necessary to crawl, roll, come up to sit or stand, or walk. This was the source of James' entirely appropriate fear of certain movements, and a clinging dependence on his mother to move him. James was chronically whining.

Prior Professional Support: At age 2 a physical therapist had miscalculated, and imposed rapid lunging movements that resulted in serious injury. Over time James' parents had made well-intentioned efforts to help him stand and walk, yet these were not effective, as he lacked the requisite learning.

Embodied, Relational Presence: I immediately noticed James' inability to transition from one position to another by himself. He was clearly aware of his weakness, lack of stability, and ineffective use of hands. He knew he could not protect himself from falls. I therefore made no attempt to "stop" his clinging and whining, and for the first Lessons allowed him to freely seek comfort from his mother, and to play familiar games. In this way I earned James' trust, and in later Lessons he was happy to be focused with me rather than with Mom.

I often learn a lot by watching how the child interacts with the parents. One day James sat on my table (with his mother), and I noticed a fascinating coping strategy: He was sitting completely rounded due to his kyphosis, with his neck and spine very "shortened". He could use his arms for play, but not for leaning or managing gravity. Through touch I could feel that he was creating a kind of "pseudo" stability by leaning into and *magnifying* his rounding through the shoulder girdle and spine — this was his way to rigidly "balance" himself to avoid falling over. While this was certainly a creative approach for sitting safely with his mother, James' arms remained "unconnected" through the shoulders, sternum, and spine. He was amplifying his rigidity, not lessening it. He was not learning to balance or transition on his own.

Yet, watching James' creative, compensatory strategy gave me the clue I needed to envision a path forward. If he can lean into and in effect magnify the kyphosis — making his spine even more rounded — maybe he could also lean "away" from the kyphosis to lessen the rounding, making his spine "longer". In other words, if he could learn to "play" with the kyphosis and make it dynamic, repeatedly exaggerating and then lessening the curvature, he could begin to differentiate his spine from his head, arms, clavicle, ribs, and so on.

Outcomes: This is exactly what happened. I invited James to explore the sensation of alternately rounding and lengthening his spine, back and forth, again and again. This created more articulation and pliability in the spine, a better sense of orientation and balance, freer breathing, and an understanding how to use his arms and hands for support. Within a few months he was able to push himself up and come to sitting (and balance on his sit bones) by himself, and to lean on one arm while playing with the other. He learned to roll back and forth from belly to back. From standing, he could bring his hands down toward the floor to protect himself when falling. This was neural plasticity in action, and wonderful to watch.

James' new-found self-orientation and balance, use of weight-shifting, and independence in movement made him more adventurous and happy. Instead of clinging and relying on his mother for every move, he started to become more of his own person. The chronic fear and whining were replaced by pleasure.

Takeaways: It can be intimidating to see a severe genetic condition or malformed body, and easy to think "there is nothing I can do". And when, as here, there was a history of injury from a prior therapy, we practitioners might be forgiven for questioning our prospects. Yet, brain plasticity allows for new learning, albeit starting with the existing neural map as presented by the client. I leveraged that map — with the clue provided by James himself via his creative coping strategy — to envision a path toward new horizons. The work was gentle and took time and patience. Rather than impose, I started where I found James, earned his trust, and then invited him to the dance and to the learning process. The result, within just months, was his empowering and pleasurable exploration of new movements and self-agency — an impressive display of neural plasticity.

⊙

Taking it One Step At a Time
Joann: Age 7 *(Sylvia)*

Diagnosis: Spastic Quadriplegia Cerebral Palsy.

Deficits: Spastic across entire body. Unable to walk, wheelchair/stroller bound. Prior attempts to use a walker were not productive. Full language intellectually, but hard to understand due to unclear diction.

Prior Professional Support: Multiple conventional therapies (without apparent outcomes); Lessons with local movement practitioners, resulting in good self-awareness and an interest in learning.

Embodied, Relational Presence: Using sight, touch, and movement I felt my way through the severe spasticity. It was evident that Joann had never learned all the movement elements requisite to becoming upright, and eventually walking. So rather than addressing walking, I started with what was here now: I focused on Lesson elements involving use of the arms, elbows, and hands, bringing them down and leaning through them for support, as small children typically learn to do. I also invited Joann to differentiate arms and legs through new movements of the spine, neck, and jaw. This had the added results of improved swallowing and diction.

Owing to her previous work with a capable movement practitioner, Joann had a good sense of self and was receptive to new learning, making my job much easier. The parents were very happy with the obvious progress. Yet, it was also clear that the level of spasticity would continue to constrain that progress. For this reason, the parents ultimately chose Selective Percutaneous Myofascial Lengthening (SPML) surgery, a procedure that treats the tight tendons associated with CP spasticity. This surgery is not always appropriate, and by itself is not a "cure". But when successful and followed up with our movement work, bigger shifts become possible. Having seen the good results of our Lessons even without the surgery, the parents decided it was a promising approach for Joann.

Returning after the SPML surgery, Joann's feet and heels came all the way flat on the ground, opening a new realm of learning opportunities. Re-visiting my earlier observations and intuitions, I took Joann through several key sequential learning elements of an infant becoming a toddler: Lying down, differentiating arms and legs, rolling, grabbing feet, flexing, crawling, and sitting. By monitoring her movements I could see that it was also essential to guide her to better organize her eyes and visual tracking as she moved, thereby developing her vestibular system and balance.

Outcomes: Over the course of multiple lessons after the SPML surgery, Joann practiced sitting, coming upright, and standing. We went back and forth from floor to standing until she was comfortable with the new movements (neural plasticity). The moment came that I sensed she was ready to take some steps. But I knew that first it was essential for her not to fear the act of falling, and in fact to experience falling as a normal aspect of movement that can be managed and safe.

I gave Joann a big pillow to fall into, and worked with her to be able to use her hands to catch herself in a fall. She took her time, but got excited and happy. She suddenly began to "leap" into the pillow, rather stiffly at first. And then she took a step or two before each next leap. She was enjoying it! That evening after the Lesson, her parents were amazed to see Joann walk across the living room unassisted, and fall onto her bed. With considerable emotion they shared the video of her first true walk. Within just a few more months, she was walking fluidly around town without assistance.

Takeaways: Many topics of this *Primer* are reflected in the story of Joann. I was very grateful for the excellent prior movement work that made her more present and receptive by the time I met her. Through my own embodied and relational presence I knew she was lacking necessary sequential learning from childhood; there was no point trying to *make* her stand, take steps, or walk. I started with her existing neural map, and was under no illusion that a miracle would be forthcoming. I humbly and curiously worked with what was present in the moment, with good (but necessarily limited) results. Yet, those results were enough to motivate the parents to choose the step of surgery, which was successful.

After the surgery, both Joann and I were ready for an entirely new adventure made possible by her reduced spasticity and greater capacity to lean into her skeleton. We went back to the basics, in effect allowing Joann to fill certain experiential gaps from her infancy and toddler years; she was creating the new neural networks necessary to get her from where she was in the moment to, ultimately, unassisted walking. At no point did I as the practitioner *impose* techniques or protocols; I continually offered an experiential learning *process*, based on where I found her in each moment, and made it exciting and fun. Joann ran with it (figuratively and literally), transforming her movement, her confidence, her pleasure, and her life.

Getting Unstuck & the Power of Collaboration
Jane: Age 2 *(Sylvia & Colleague)*

Diagnosis: Mild cerebral palsy and developmental delays.

Deficits: A casual observer might have thought that Jane was doing pretty well. She was able to stand, but only when placed standing and then leaning against something or someone. She could sit, but only if someone first sat her up. She could "walk", but only when supported by adult hands. She was entirely unable to transition herself to and between these positions, and this lack of self-agency made her highly insecure, unhappy, whiny, and distrustful of strangers.

Prior Professional Support: A physical therapist had showed Jane's mother how to "do" exercises with Jane at home to help her walk, but Jane did not have the requisite learning to make sense of it; the exercises were thus frustrating and unproductive for both child and mother. The parents found a local movement practitioner who did excellent work, but he was stymied by Jane's whining refusal to be touched. When this practitioner could not find a way in, he referred Jane to me for a consult and supervision.

Embodied, Relational Presence: I first felt into Jane's extreme unhappiness; she could not shift positions by herself, and yet did not want anyone showing her how. She did not like to be touched, but I quickly felt with my hands her tense trunk, tight lower back, and lack of articulation and pliability in the spine. I saw that Jane had zero awareness of her pelvis, or that it was connected to her spine or limbs, or that she had the power to move it. She therefore had no way to protect herself — if she were not properly supported she would fall over like a tree. This made her understandably insecure, fearful, and whiny. In a word, she felt powerless, and not surprisingly distrusted strangers. I fully understood why my colleague had "hit a wall" and made the referral.

I readily envisioned that Jane's path forward was through her awareness and activation of the pelvis. Yet, Jane's limited and engrained neural map was indeed hard to find a way into. So I stepped back and gave ample time for Jane to get to know and trust me. I let her play with toys and her mother while I gently "sneaked in" here and there to touch and move her.

Over several Lessons Jane noticed small changes in her movements, and let me touch her more and more without complaint. That is, she awoke to the learning opportunity being offered. As her innate capacity for neural plasticity was activated, it became interesting or even pleasurable to her, and she decided to trust and let it happen. By our third set of Lessons, Jane was at ease with the work, and had also warmed up to the colleague who had originally referred her to me. That colleague and I were now fully collaborating as a "tag team" to maximize Jane's Lessons and optimize her developmental trajectory.

Outcomes: Through our Lessons Jane learned that she had a pelvis, that it was connected to her spine, and that she could move that pelvis in various directions. As she became more oriented to her body, she experimented rolling "into" and "over" her pelvis forward and back, left and right. This led to a more articulated and pliable spine, freer limbs, and far less tension throughout her body. She could use her hands and arms to push and protect. She no longer feared falling. The more she moved, the more self-confident and happy she became. She was funny and expressive. The whining was gone.

By age 3, and after less than a year of Lessons, Jane had learned to transition by herself, including rolling, crawling, sitting, standing, climbing onto furniture, and walking without assistance. She still would not climb stairs, until her arrival at one of our last Lessons together: She took a moment to consider the stairs leading up to my office, and then walked right up.

Takeaways: As noted earlier in this *Primer*, there are times for all of us when the learning process seems stuck. Jane's excellent local movement practitioner recognized this moment and sought a consult and supervision, which led to a powerful collaboration and remarkable results for the client in a very short period of time. Both of us practitioners necessarily started with Jane's rather cramped neural map at the outset, yet could envision a fluid pelvis and all that would follow. But first, we gently and patiently earned Jane's trust and found our way in. We understood that imposing exercises or continuing to "hold" Jane in various positions would not evoke the learning process (it was key that the parents fully cooperated with our approach). We didn't address "walking" in any direct way at all, but allowed it to evolve naturally through her internal, native neural plasticity. Together we practitioners, parents, and most importantly Jane herself danced — or should I say "walked" — with considerable pleasure into a new neural reality.

SEEING BEYOND THE OBVIOUS

Changing the World With a Single Finger
Julio: Age 9 *(Kerstin)*

Diagnosis: ADHD, learning disabilities, behavioral disorders.

Deficits: Difficulty focusing attention, at both home and school. Aggressive towards classmates, social misconduct. Could not use pen or pencil effectively to write, due to use of extreme force.

Prior Professional Support: For three years Julio had attended a special education school for children with learning disabilities and behavioral problems. He had received occupational therapy during that time to help him learn to use pen and pencil effectively, with limited success.

Embodied, Relational Presence: Feeling into Julio beyond his outward behaviors, I could sense that he was a very sweet child. I became quite curious about the quality of his ADHD, and particularly his aggression. What might cause him to be so forceful, both with other people and with his attempts at writing? I wondered whether this might be an unconscious compensation for some sense of inadequacy or failure. I quickly intuited that Julio's inability to control a pencil or pen was my entry point to his developmental impasse and learning process.

So, in our first Lesson I had Julio write his name on a piece of paper with a pencil. He used so much force that his jagged writing indented the soft wood of the table below. I noted that the fingertips of his clenched writing hand were white from lack of blood flow. Julio held his breath with every letter he wrote, further reducing his sensitivity and control. I examined the mobility of each finger on his writing hand, and felt that his ring finger was even stiffer than the other fingers. I then examined the fingers of the other hand, where the ring finger was more normal.

I wondered aloud about the difference between the two ring fingers, and I had Julio compare for himself the feeling of movement in each finger. He quickly felt the difference, got very curious, and experimented with both hands. He almost immediately adjusted the dynamic of the ring finger of his writing hand to match the other finger. He made this change on his own, as he became aware of his hands and fingers in a very new way.

I then asked Julio to write his name again, which he did with great ease and without the prior forcefulness. Julio saw that he could be a quick learner, and was quite pleased with himself. His father, who had been watching all this, was almost unbelieving: "We've spent three years trying to get him to use a pen properly, and now after only a few minutes he writes as though there was never a problem!"

Outcomes: After just a single Lesson, Julio had learned how to use his hand normally. This triggered a cascade effect. Julio's entire nervous system reorganized itself as soon as the unnecessary excitation of the writing hand was resolved. His breathing became full and easy, giving him more awareness and control in each moment. His mother reported that Julio's new-found self-confidence had transformed his affect and behavior: "Julio has become such a lovely boy — really easy to deal with and helping at home on his own initiative wherever he can. This is completely new to us — we had never met him like this." Six months later, the parents were told to take Julio out of the special education school, as his grades and behaviors had so improved that he no longer needed any special support.

I learned only later that Julio's stiff ring finger had been completely severed in an accident when he was a baby. A skilled surgeon sewed it back on with excellent physiological success, and without any visible scar. However, it was now apparent that the trauma had persisted, affecting Julio's perception and use of his hand, and by extension his coping behaviors. Years later he was still holding his breath and clenching, presumably an unconscious, self-protective reflex. This had been his neural map since infancy, resulting in lowered sensitivity and control in all his daily activities. I surmise that Julio's understandable feelings of inadequacy in turn led to "acting out" aggressively. That is, unconsciously Julio had been seeking self-empowerment and agency through sheer force, which was one thing he could do well. Now, his innate capacity for neural plasticity gave him an entirely new sense of self-agency and power, displacing the habituated strategies that were no longer necessary.

Takeaways: The story of Julio's finger illustrates many key concepts of this *Primer*. I used my relational presence to see past the outward ADHD behaviors and ask: "I wonder . . ." This spaciousness allowed me to tune into a seemingly small, yet crucial, neural impasse: Julio's lack of free movement in a finger, and the associated clenching and held breath. At the time I was not aware of the earlier trauma. Yet, I could "feel" that starting with this portion of Julio's existing neural map might open up new vistas. He gladly accepted my invitation to dance with his own fingers, and without any directive from me quickly created a new neural "map" for his finger and hand. This "small" learning was the missing prerequisite needed to dissolve the impasse, leading to a remarkable transformation in Julio's sense of self-worth, self-confidence, and empowerment. Starting with the very first Lesson, and over the next several months, the cascade of new neural networks had displaced his old behaviors and limitations. He changed his finger and changed his world.

Don't Judge the Book By Its Cover
Josephine: Age 3½ *(Sylvia)*

Diagnosis: Rare genetic disorder resulting in a disproportionately large and heavy head, small body, and global developmental challenges. The neurologist advised the parents that Josephine would not achieve normal function, or likely live for very long.

Deficits: No eye contact, with wandering eyes that could not focus. Right side of body had not "mapped" and was not used. Could not control her head, could not roll, and was chronically fussy with random wriggling movements.

Prior Professional Support: Josephine did not like or benefit from prior attempts at physical therapy. Her parents later found an excellent movement practitioner who was able to evoke Josephine's interest in learning, which set the stage for me to help her deepen the learning process.

Embodied, Relational Presence: I quickly observed that Josephine had no concept of focusing her vision or managing the weight of her head; it was as though the eyes and head were entirely disconnected from the rest of her. Through touch and movement, I also understood the severe lack of right-side awareness, as well as the compensatory but ineffective use of the left side. I necessarily started with her existing neural map, but was already forming a larger vision: How can I help Josephine experience that her head is not a separate entity, but is attached to a spine, which is attached to a pelvis? Such awareness would allow the possibility that, by learning minimal weight shifting through the torso, she could control her large head and use her entire body to move in new ways.

Outcomes: In light of Josephine's existing map, my early Lessons emphasized visual clues and sounds, to help her better organize her eyes and focus on the world around her. I worked around her face and mouth to increase awareness of the head, and its connection to her body. She started to become comfortable lying on her belly. She could then feel weight shifting: Again and again, she experienced that her head could now roll over the left arm, then over the right arm. She eventually "got" this ability to transition (neural plasticity), and was able to roll on her own from side to side.

Josephine's parents took her home and reported that she was "rolling all over the place". This was a huge deal for Josephine (and her parents), and the beginning of more rapid shifts. Josephine could now make full eye contact. She could be on her belly and lift her heavy head. She could keep her head up while sitting. She had use of the right side of her body, and could coordinate both left and right (such as moving toys from hand to hand across the midline). Her new sense of empowerment through movement transformed her prior whining into smiles and laughter. And her curiosity continues to grow.

Takeaways: Despite her severe challenges, Josephine proved herself to be a fast and able learner. It would have been easy to discount her potential for change, as the neurologist may have done. Just looking at her huge, heavy head might have intimidated or discouraged some helpers. Yet, by tuning in to her existing map I was able to envision a possible expansion of the neural territory through integrating the eyes, head, spine, and pelvis. As I "danced" with Josephine toward this possibility, she readily formed new neural networks, and loved the sense of empowerment. I can't know where her next neural horizon will take her, but I am confident Josephine will continue to learn and progress.

SLOWING IT ALL DOWN

Unveiling the Inner Landscape
Jess: Age 2 *(Sylvia & Supervision Colleagues)*

Diagnosis: Cerebral palsy. Nonverbal.

Deficits: Jess' extremities were rigid and spastic, with minimal use of the extensor or flexor muscles. He had no awareness of his spine or its connection with the rest of his body; he could not bend or make much use of his limbs, could not get himself up or down, or shift himself into sitting or standing. Instead of crawling he improvised a kind of "hopping." He constantly wiggled with rapid, rigid, staccato movements. Jess' parents had tried to "walk" him, but stopped upon realizing the danger of him falling without the ability to protect himself. He also had feeding and chewing problems.

Prior Professional Support: Neither physical therapy, occupational therapy, nor speech therapy had resulted in any evident shifts. In their search for a new approach, the parents found one of my Professional Supervision Intensives and enrolled Jess as a client. Over three days he received nine Lessons, from me and six other certified practitioners under my supervision.

Embodied, Relational Presence: Jess was a lively ball of non-stop energy, constantly smiling, waving, and wiggling. He simply did not slow down, and always gave the appearance of being "ahead of himself". Our group surmised that he had learned to connect with those around him through his skill as an "entertainer" — he would entertain us, and in return we would attend to him. We quickly realized that our vision for Jess necessarily started with inviting him to slow down enough to become aware of his internal reality, the prerequisite to new learning. Yet, Jess had never experienced this, and in fact his habituated, automatic coping strategy prevented it. So how to go about inviting him into his own inner world?

Thanks to our own ability to slow way down, we practitioners were able to meet Jess where he was, but without matching his frenetic activity ourselves. Rather than join in the "entertainment", we used eye contact, voice, gentle movements, and just our very "slow" presence to invite him to shift his own familiar pattern. We were creating a "container" for Jess to feel safe doing something different.

Outcomes: By the third day, Jess "got it" (neural plasticity), and his shift was palpable to the point of dramatic. He was suddenly paying attention to himself — his body parts, his movements, his sensations. Rapid-fire entertainment had been replaced by a slow and soft attentiveness. His entire demeanor was transformed. It was as if he had discovered a different universe, and he was fascinated. This was such a radical and beautiful change that it brought tears to both parents and practitioners.

Not coincidentally, with his new self-awareness Jess quickly attained more movement in his spine, freer limbs, and a mobile pelvis. He began rolling. The parents immediately understood what had happened, and shifted out of their own habitual ways of interacting with Jess.

In periodic Lessons with me over the next several months, Jess truly engaged with the "dance". He expected and welcomed me to guide him to new opportunities, which he embraced with curiosity and enthusiasm; he quickly translated my verbal invitations into movement. He could transition between squatting and standing, crawl up stairs, walk on knees, and began actively experimenting with verbalizing and communication. His fine motor skills developed rapidly. While he could still at times fall back on the old neural patterns of frenetic entertainment and "hopping", his new networks were "firing and wiring together" and gaining primacy. Changes kept coming more rapidly, all made possible by his receptive presence to an inner world previously invisible to him.

Takeaways: As Dr. Feldenkrais pointed out, when we live our lives doing what we think is expected of us, rather than deeply feeling and knowing ourselves and acting from that inner strength, we will not be whole. This is a challenge faced by many adults. In the case of Jess, our first and necessary step was inviting him to realize that he even had an inner landscape, a territory that is actually more interesting and rewarding than his habituated frenetic coping strategy. Because the practitioners in our supervision group knew how to be with Jess from their own embodied, relational presence, Jess felt he was being held in a safe container. He could then choose for himself to accept our invitations and explore this fascinating new inner world, leaving behind the customary distractions. As generally happens in our work, the client's innate capacity for neural plasticity led to a cascade of multiple and interwoven shifts in awareness, perception, and action — both internal and external.

The Power of Doing Nothing
Jennifer: Age 4 *(Kerstin)*

Diagnosis: Cerebral palsy and epilepsy. Left side of body particularly spastic. Uncoordinated eye movements had resulted in multiple eye operations.

Deficits: Jennifer would throw her head abruptly and at high speed in different directions. At rest, her head was stretched out backwards. She grabbed people or objects with great force, and pulled so as not to fall over. She made little effort to use her eyes or hands to manipulate objects, or to support herself. She had no interest in her own feet. Crawling, standing up, and walking were not possible due to her lack of self-awareness and sharp, excited movements.

Prior Professional Support: In physical therapy Jennifer's legs had been "trained" by forcing them into extreme and tense stretches to achieve "standing". However, she pushed herself up on her toes and was unable to lower her heels. Walking was not possible, and would be dangerous in any event as she could not use her arms and hands to protect herself in a fall.

Embodied, Relational Presence: Although her spasticity and vision issues were certainly conspicuous, what first caught my attention about Jennifer was her skill "talking". She had a knack for unusual statements and charming questions that would often elicit laughter from her audience, which she enjoyed very much. I also was impressed by her extraordinary power of hearing; she could readily and accurately repeat and play with the sounds she heard. However, her keen talent to hear and talk did not translate to an ability to *listen*. For example, Jennifer would ask a lot of questions, but without necessarily waiting for or absorbing an answer. She could not remain silent or be still while others were talking. I began to see the developmental gap and impasse that I might help her address, through *the power of silence and doing nothing.*

I challenged Jennifer to a game: I would count out loud for ten seconds, during which time she could not speak, move, stretch, or even tense a muscle. She had to be completely still and quiet. Such a concept of stillness and silence had never occurred to Jennifer, and it certainly was not part of her neural map as to how to interact with the world and get attention. We played this game a number of times until Jennifer "won". When she did, and saw that she had the power to control herself for ten whole seconds, it was palpable how her self-awareness and self-confidence shifted. Realizing that she could have self-agency over her body and behaviors made her proud and joyous.

Outcomes: Jennifer's new-found agency and curiosity created a cascade effect. She quickly got curious and began exploring hands, feet, and the focused vision necessary to make use of her body in the world; she started looking around and coordinating with her limbs. Her head movements became more steady and measured. She experimented with her hands and pushing, and became more balanced in the act of standing as well as lowering herself down. Instead of the habitual and continual jerking and grabbing and chattering, she became more inwardly attentive to how she *felt*, what she might want to *do,* and where she might want to go *go.*

Simply put, Jennifer's ability to quiet herself and "do nothing" directly empowered her to autonomously explore her inner and outer worlds. Her talent for *getting* attention was placed in service of *giving* attention to herself. She could then translate her talent for "hearing" into the ability to listen to herself and her body. Her pleasure in evoking laughter gave way to the pleasure of empowered self-agency. Her grabby dependence on others became differentiation and self-confidence in autonomous, coordinated movement.

At the end of one Lesson Jennifer noticed a light switch on the wall. Entirely on her own she had the idea to stand herself up against the wall, walk sideways along the wall without assistance (by necessity coordinating arms and legs), and reach the light switch with her hand to turn it on and off (requiring her to precisely coordinate her eyes and focus). This small yet momentous act confirmed the profound shift in her developmental trajectory. Jennifer's mother was amazed.

Takeaways: Jennifer's habituated neural map had limited her to using clever chatter and laughter to "control" her environment and create love and safety. Through my relational presence I sensed into the larger and interconnected picture of her body, intellect, emotional affect, and coping strategies, and could envision a path beyond. She had never been given the option to slow down, indeed to simply stop her patterned behavior, in a safe and loving (and fun) way. Jennifer then discovered that silence and stillness were not only within her power, but empowering. And they still provided her with the love and safety she needed. Her native neural plasticity was activated, triggering a rapid and self-reinforcing cascade of curiosity, pleasure, and learning. Jennifer's case neatly illustrates the power of creating a "safe container" based on an unhurried and heartfelt presence, within which practitioner and child jointly "dance" into entirely new neural territory and potential.

●

When Parents Say "Yes" To Slowing Down Johnny: Age 3½ *(Sylvia)*

Many parents have fully explored multiple treatment options before they come to us, perceiving that their child may need something different. One such case is that of Johnny, a boy with cerebral palsy, missing brain matter, and numerous deficits. He had been engaged in multiple and daily therapies to address speech, vision, and movement. He could not transition by himself between positions, and could not squat, stand, or walk. He received quite rigid, even forceful "training". Despite all these interventions, the parents realized Johnny was not progressing well, much less thriving. They came to me.

In our first visit I immediately noted Johnny's very "flat" emotional affect, and lack of any evident pleasure in life. If he had been an adult, I might have called him resigned, defeated, or withdrawn. As I introduced myself it was evident that Johnny was not at all happy about yet another therapy session with yet another therapist. Through touch and observation, I realized that he was, in fact, overwhelmed. Johnny simply could not take in all the stimuli, but neither would he object to it. He was being an obedient "good boy" doing what he was told. Hence the "dullness" in his affect.

I discussed with the parents the possibility that all the well-intentioned efforts to "impose" learning on Johnny were instead "turning off" his innate curiosity and desire to learn. I proposed, and they agreed, that we try to "wake up" his neural plasticity by doing the exact opposite of what, by now, he was expecting.

First, I slowed everything way down, got connected and relational, and invited Johnny to explore leisurely but intentional movement. There was no demand, pressure, or expectation. Johnny quickly noted this change in the attitude of the adults. In this new spaciousness there was room for *him*. He became more interested in me, and attentive to the movements.

Second, given his flat affect, I knew it was important for Johnny to experience some self-agency, as well as joy in movement. I got playful, and said: "I know you don't want me telling you what to do. But if you want to get rid of me, you are going to have to push me away!" Now I really had Johnny's attention, and he would have pushed me right then and there, but did not yet know how. So we played a pushing game, and he slowly but surely learned to use legs and feet, arms and hands, to push me. He got curious and engaged, and his "flatness" disappeared. He discovered his own power. He started **giggling** and having fun with the movements.

After several days of Lessons, Johnny had become far more curious, adventurous, and communicative. He was expressing feelings and joy, and wanted more contact with his parents. At the third day, he let go of his mother's hand, took his very first independent steps, and then lowered himself down to squatting. None of this had seemed possible just days earlier. Johnny showed genuine pleasure in his accomplishment. The parents were astonished. And, shortly after these Lessons, the parents reported that "Johnny is walking all over the place."

Takeaways: The case of Johnny reminds us that, at least in our profession, *less* really can be *more*. All the therapists who had been working with him were no doubt doing excellent work. Cumulatively, however, that daily demand was overwhelming his system. Rather than creating new neural networks, Johnny was capitulating to forces beyond his control. His natural desire for learning was not activated, and in fact was defended and blocked. It required surprisingly little in the way of slow, spacious, and relational Experiential Movement Lessons to reverse that defensive posture, and engage Johnny's native capacity for neural plasticity and pleasurable, powerful learning. He learned to walk without any "training" or demand from me.

Saying "No" to a Parent Who Chooses Not to Slow Down
Jill: Age 12 *(Sylvia)*

The flip side of Johnny's story is the parent who chooses not to slow down. One example was the 12-year old Jill, who had cerebral palsy, was nonverbal, and was cognitively far behind for her age level. She engaged in spectrum-like repetitive behaviors. She could not crawl, or put herself in a sitting position, or stand or walk. Interestingly, once placed in a sitting position, she was able to bring her pelvis over her knees (for kneeling). I used this ability as my entry point, envisioning that I might elicit a new learning experience of balancing on the knees, which could lead to free "knee-walking" and, eventually, far more mobility and self-agency. At least, that was my vision for Jill.

Yet, even before I was able to fully connect with Jill, her father proved to be a challenging "gatekeeper". He was a complex collection of contradictions. On the one hand, he was quite anxious and came to me admitting that he was "looking for a miracle". On the other hand, he was deeply religious and had faith that God would provide for Jill without any human intervention. He claimed to want a "professional" to be working with Jill, yet during the Lessons he made non-stop efforts to tell me what to do, and how, and when. Jill had been receiving a very rigid, "mechanical" therapy without good outcomes, yet the father did not seem interested in my explanations of why Jill might benefit from the more relational and fluid dance that our work provides.

Despite some clear shifts in Jill over our several Lessons together, the father seemed unimpressed and kept referring to the old therapy, which in my view likely would set back Jill if she continued it. At our last session the father insisted that I provide him with "exercises" that he could "give" Jill between visits. He was quite upset when I declined, not accepting my explanation that, in Jill's case, such an imposition likely would be counter-productive to the learning process that she was now engaged in. I instead gave the father several names of wonderful movement practitioners in his local area, and suggested that Jill would benefit from their regular support before our next appointment, which was scheduled for a few months later.

After several weeks I checked in with the father, and learned that he had made no effort to schedule local Lessons for Jill. He was opting to continue the previous "mechanical" therapy. Yet, he still wanted to keep Jill's upcoming appointment with me. I thought this likely to be counterproductive: I might well have to "start from scratch" each time Jill came back to me. Worse, Jill would be getting mixed and frustrating signals from the very different approaches. And, the father and I would no doubt continue to find each other unaccommodating. As much as I wanted the best for Jill, I decided my further involvement was not in her best interest. I accepted the father's choice of modality without argument, reminding him of the local movement practitioners available to him, and suggesting he pick just one modality to pursue at a time. And with that closure, I cancelled our appointment.

Takeaways: We mentioned earlier the importance of acknowledging when we seem to be "spinning our wheels" as practitioners, owing to "external" factors. I did my best for Jill, and pointed out her meaningful shifts, but that was not enough for her father. I referred him to my excellent colleagues in his immediate area, but he did not follow up, instead opting for the familiar, albeit clearly unsuccessful, "mechanical" therapy. As concerned as I was for Jill, I deemed that it would have been worse to subject her to continuing conflict and confusion around her father's pursuit of competing modalities. This was a case where the client's native learning process would not be supported, or have a chance to unfold, at home between Lessons. Moreover, I would be denying space to another client who might more readily embrace our work. So I said "no".

| RELATIONAL PRESENCE IN REAL TIME |

The Leisurely Unfolding Moment
Jackie: Age 15 months
(Sylvia & Supervision Colleagues)

Diagnosis: Premature birth with cerebral palsy. Brain shunt required due to meningitis contracted in hospital.

Deficits: Tiny size, as if half her age. Visual impairment. No head control or ability to roll. Despite a "floppy" head, tremendous tightness around the jaw and mouth. Could not latch onto the bottle, and was not able to eat normally.

Prior Professional Support: An excellent movement practitioner had previously evoked Jackie's curiosity and interest in learning. This snapshot comes from her slightly later participation as a child client in two of my Professional Supervision Intensives, over back-to-back weekends. In each, Jackie received three lessons per day over three days (a total of 6 days and 18 Lessons), from me and 12 other certified practitioners under my supervision.

Embodied, Relational Presence: Owing to her prior Lessons with the movement practitioner, Jackie was already alert and curious. The collective vision of our Supervision group was to improve and integrate her visual capacity and head control, which would lead to many new learning opportunities. Yet, these were precisely her deficits — the inability to use her eyes or head to track the world around her. The solution to this dilemma? Our profound and accommodating relational presence, with continuing invitations and feedback, in "real time".

We started with Jackie's existing neural map, requiring that we slow ourselves way down to her speed, meeting her where her limited visual capacity could register what we were doing. Very gently and unhurriedly we used motion, sound, smiles, and toys to invite her to track her own body and the world around her. We did not impose ourselves, and gave ample time and space for Jackie's nervous system to receive each new invitation and sensation, which in turn allowed Jackie to notice and explore at her own pace. She began focusing on things going on around her, and use her head and eyes to track.

I also invited Jackie to become aware of the sensations of her mouth, tongue, cheeks, and gums. This in turn evoked new awareness of both the inside and the outside of the head, and their connection with the neck and spine. Such awareness is a prerequisite to learning to roll.

Outcomes: Over just these several days, Jackie learned to precisely track the details of the world around her, and the relationship between her eyes, head, and spine. She learned head control and discovered rolling. She could even roll to her belly and then lift her head to carefully follow what was going on around her! Not coincidentally, she started feeding more, and more easily. This rapid transformation in her dynamic participation with the world took our breath away.

Takeaways: Given her young age and deficits, Jackie could not re-organize herself without skilled yet unhurried guidance. Because the practitioners in our group were able to slow way down and patiently meet her where we found her in each moment, Jackie's nervous system could *receive* our undivided relational presence and the safe container we created for her. She could *receive* our gentle invitations to organize her visual capacity. She could *receive* the new sensations of movement inside and outside her head. Through this unforced, organic upwelling of awareness, Jackie experienced for herself interesting new uses of her head, neck, and spine. She was now fully engaged in the learning process that we practitioners had elicited, leading to better and better body control, growing curiosity, and a dynamic participation in the world around her. These several days with Jackie offered a moving demonstration of our *marvelous métier* of relational presence with the client in "real time", and once again the beauty of how as practitioners we *embody, envision, elicit,* and *empower.*

⊙

Whispering to the Whole Child
Jojo: Age 10 months *(Kerstin)*

Diagnosis: Birth trauma (umbilical cord wrapped around the neck several times), resulting in lack of oxygen, hypotension, listlessness.

Deficits: Inability to swallow (feeding tube required through nose) and labored, wheezing breathing. Mouth was constantly open, and both the nose tube and mucous made breathing more difficult. Could not move her head, and her eyes were always closed as if sleeping. Trunk and extremities bloated. Largely motionless.

Prior Professional Support: Various therapies and rehabilitation efforts, including specialists working with her swallowing. Limited changes.

Embodied, Relational Presence: Her parents arrived focused on Jojo's impaired swallowing and eating. But what immediately caught my attention was Jojo's small motionless head, her comparatively puffy body, and her "sleepy" lack of contact and awareness. I first felt her neck muscles, which were extremely tight, and noted the complete immobility of her shoulder girdle and spine. Jojo had not yet learned that she had separate yet interconnected parts of a body, much less how to move and use them. In fact, her neural map was frozen in a holding pattern. She had no *motivation* to move. Some might have been quick to label the mostly motionless Jojo as a "lazy" or "apathetic" or "disabled" infant. How to find a way to engage her learning process?

I necessarily started with the existing neural map. I knew that Jojo's sense of hearing through the ears would require the *least* movement of her body, and I was curious whether she would react to sound. But I also wanted to test this in a very *relational* manner that had meaning for her. So, I put her mother on Jojo's left and her father on her right, and had them alternately whisper Jojo's name into her ears. Jojo promptly began to turn her head very slightly, and then further and further, to one side and then the other as her name was called. Under her closed eyelids there were small signs of eye movement. We had found a way in.

Continuing with this gentle approach, Jojo's previously tight neck and motionless head now became "useful" things that she could use to seek out meaningful connections with her loving parents. Her nervous system "woke up" to new possibilities, and her shoulder girdle got involved in the increasing movements. Mobility in the spine followed. As these movements and body parts became more coordinated and integrated, Jojo moved more and more easily, and on her own initiative. Her neural plasticity was activated and she was embracing the learning process at a rapid pace.

Outcomes: Over a series of Lessons, Jojo's experience of differentiation and mobility in the neck, shoulder, and spine quickly affected the rest of her body. Her eyes opened, and she kept them open more and more, as she moved her head to view her surroundings. Her breathing became freer, and she could swallow. During one Lesson she suddenly was able to roll to the side and then on her stomach, support herself on her elbows and forearms, and immediately afterwards vertically align her head with her stretched arms. The prior hypotension was gone. She had become a curious, motivated, and active infant.

Shortly after our Lessons began, Jojo no longer required her feeding tube, and the mucous and wheezing stopped. The parents were pleasantly surprised that this outcome – which was their reason for coming to me in the first place – was not accomplished by any direct work on her swallowing, but rather by their loving whispers in her ears.

Takeaways: Dr. Feldenkrais noted that "the whole person has to move", and he meant physiologically, emotionally, and intellectually – all of our parts work together and are mutually interdependent. Jojo was not a "lazy" or "apathetic" baby, but rather a baby who, owing to her severe birth trauma, could not activate her learning process on her own. She needed the practitioner's vision of a path beyond her currently frozen neural map – as well as the relational, loving invitations of her parents — to go down that path and engage with her world in a new way. Jojo's empowerment was truly the joint success of the practitioner's embodied presence, devoted caregivers, and Jojo's own native capacity for neural plasticity and learning.

ORGANIZED IMPROVISATION

Curling Into Connection
Jeremy: Age 12 *(Kerstin)*

Diagnosis: Cerebral palsy, epilepsy, and autism spectrum.

Deficits: Hyperactive and uncontrolled actions, interrupted breathing, and repetitive humming sounds or screeching. Biting of the hands and wrists. Extreme tension in jaw, neck, and throat. Could eat and manipulate objects with his hands, yet under high agitation and often lacking control. Able to walk but with an unsteady gait. As he could not organize his extremities quickly enough to protect himself, he was at risk of injury from falling.

Prior Professional Support: Acupuncture had been somewhat helpful in calming Jeremy's nervous system.

Embodied, Relational Presence: Like many people on the spectrum, Jeremy lived in his own world, and was easily overwhelmed by unfamiliar or unpleasant sensations, and unwelcome interventions. Before I could even begin connecting, I realized that his sensitivity required me to deepen my self-awareness. I needed to monitor and take responsibility for my attitude and intention in every unfolding moment, and the possible impact of even my smallest actions. Jeremy would immediately know if I were using my intentionality, hands, and touch in a forcing, manipulative, or judgmental manner. Above all else, his nervous system needed to experience acceptance, love, and safety. Under these circumstances, how best to invite Jeremy to "dance"?

In my mind's eye — this was not a planned or rational act on my part — I envisioned Jeremy in the fetal position. This is the universal self-protective flexion movement of humans: In the safety of the womb this is how we grow; after birth, when we feel sick or sad we may retreat to our bed and curl up until we recover; when falling or fighting we can instinctively roll up and into ourself to lesson the blow. It is a safe, soothing, and ultimately restorative position.

It felt right to me to explore this image, so I considered whether Jeremy had the requisite movement skills to curl himself up. Could his eyes look down and head drop? Could the shoulder girdle and sternum sink inward? The cervical and lumbar vertebrae round? The limbs and extremities fold? I spent a number of Lessons with Jeremy offering experiences of each of these elements, simply by being present with him. I modeled curiosity and exploration, but did not cajole, impose, or expect. From my relational presence, I followed Jeremy's lead, bearing witness to his self-observation and growing self-awareness.

Outcomes: Through this patient process of unforced exploration, Jeremy became more calm, receptive, and relational. My heartfelt connection was reciprocated, as he experienced my acceptance and the safety of our time together. The Lesson arrived in which all the "curling" elements came together. Jeremy softened and almost melted into me. It was as if we became one, curling into a single ball of safe and soothing motion. Together we moved on the table in a simple, yet profound communion. For at least this moment in time, Jeremy was not hyperactive, agitated, or defended. He experienced himself safely and quietly in close relationship with another. As importantly, he had autonomously created new neural networks for curling, flexing, and extending through his body, which will allow far more ease and control of movement over time. In my subsequent Lessons with Jeremy, he appeared to be holding on to the experience, and remained very welcoming of our connection. He was calmer, more focused, and his movement and gait much improved.

Takeaways: I had no tangible clue where my vision for Jeremy might lead. I nevertheless followed my intuition and heart, rather than some intellectual selection from the Lesson Repertoire. Over time I created spaciousness, modeled without demand, and continually monitored my own inner landscape to avoid any sense of expectation or forcing. The process allowed for a joint experience of trust and safety, leading to new and vital neural networks for Jeremy.

The Power of Joy
Jack: Age 12 *(Sylvia)*

Diagnosis: Autism Spectrum.

Deficits: Mostly nonverbal, with communication challenges; behavioral / social awkwardness; flat emotional affect; tight musculature throughout body, with particularly tense hands, wrists, ankles, neck, and jaw.

Prior Professional Support: Special Education programs; Lessons with his local movement practitioners.

Embodied, Relational Presence: This was my first introduction to Jack. Using sight, touch, and movement I tuned into Jack's tense musculature, and how he was not aware of his skeleton as a source of support. He was not only uncomfortable in his own body, but as a result was also "flat" on the emotional, feeling level. I sensed that Jack simply was not accustomed to experiencing pleasure, much less *embodied* pleasure.

In this first visit with Jack many elements of the Lesson Repertoire could have been supportive. Yet, I intuited that in this moment he might make best use of the simple experience of bodily and emotional pleasure through movement. I immediately saw and felt the image of going back in time and allowing Jack to be a small child rolling around on the floor, feeling joy.

Outcomes: I quickly realized Jack had never integrated the "simple" head, eye, and pelvis coordination needed to initiate rolling. I joined Jack on the floor and invited him to experience this coordination for himself. We played with the most simple form of rolling — like a cylinder, or sausage. It was hard for him to grasp how to do the minimal weight shifts and use together his eyes, head, and pelvis to create the roll. I continued patiently to invite him to join me. He finally "got it" (neural plasticity) and started giggling. As we rolled around together he could not stop laughing from sheer joy. His mother was deeply moved by this dramatic shift in Jack's movement and affect.

As the Lesson time came to end, Jack refused to stop rolling and laughing. He was obviously loving his empowerment. How to bring the session to a close and greet my next client? I invited Jack to use his new-found and joyful body awareness as an intentional and pleasurable way to say goodbye. Together we rolled right out of the room, giggling all the way. I gave Jack a farewell hug, and greeted my next client. Outside, Jack continued to roll around in the hallway for a short while, exploring his new and very fun neural networks.

Takeaways: On one level, this spontaneous Experiential Movement Lesson was an important step toward shifting Jack's physical and emotional tightness and holding. Rather than "intellectually" choose one of the many possible Lessons that could have been relevant to Jack's needs, I honored a deeper intuition and vision. My attuned, patient invitations to new awareness eventually led Jack to literally roll into new neural networks — he learned that through movement he can experience his body, his feelings, and the world around him in wonderful new ways. He was empowered not only in the moment, but also to continue building on this new self-confidence. On another level, it was a remarkable communion among practitioner, client, and parent; as a result of embodied and relational presence, together we created communication, awareness, and joy through movement.

A FINAL NOTE
Science, Toolbox & Art Form

We have now delivered our main message: Whatever our experience or skill level as practitioners, we can continue learning to better move *with* the Child With Special Needs. We can slow down and deepen our awareness, sensitivity, embodiment, presence, and vision. We can enliven and elevate our translation of potent Lesson elements from the rich Repertoire. We are of service to these great kids whenever we have integrated for ourself the learning that we want to offer them. In short, *we empower ourselves to empower the child.*

Along the way, our personal *embodiment:*

- ✓ *Generates* humility, curiosity, and relational presence in each unfolding moment with the child. These carry us beyond mere techniques and recipes — and offer our biggest gifts to our clients;

- ✓ *Empowers* us to let go of any particularized preconceptions, expectations, and agendas. We get out of our own way, allowing each child's native learning *process* to unfold on its own rich terms and timing;

- ✓ *Engages* us in a heartfelt, spacious, *joint* adventure with each child. We dance *with* the client, following each other's lead as we traverse the unfolding neural territory toward each new developmental horizon;

- ✓ *Builds* our self-confidence and skill translating and transmitting our awareness into each client relationship;

- ✓ *Inoculates* us from stress, anxiety, and demand (whether from our clients or ourselves), and prevents our own eventual burnout. By embracing the largely unscripted *process,* we need not pretend to be the "manager", "fixer", "hero", or "miracle worker";

- ✓ *Leads* us to seek out and grow with professional supervision and continuing education, giving us new perspectives and creative energy; and

- ✓ *Keeps* us sane, vital, and good-humored in the midst of our wonderful yet often challenging work with the superb kids and caregivers. We thrive personally and professionally.

These are enduring benefits. Even though each of us authors has been practicing and teaching movement work for 25+ years, we are still energized, passionate, and learning every day. We continue to prioritize our exploration of the Lesson Repertoire, deepening our awareness and personal organization (and thus our service to our clients). We regularly get new ideas and perspectives from our colleagues, and seek out seasoned, masterful practitioners who provide the reality-checks we need to hone and elevate our skill. All of this helps keep us sharp and vital, taking us in creative and effective directions with our clients. *Each new day our work is fresh and exciting.*

If you have read this far, you may have already gathered that neither of us puts much stock in "official" educational or professional titles by themselves. To paraphrase Dr. Feldenkrais, it is our personal presence, sensitivity, vision, and vital relationships with ourselves and our clients that make all the difference, not the piece of paper we hang on the wall.

> *Our sustained professional success as movement practitioners is not because we "give lessons", or have a good "technique", or because we write a particular certification title after our name.*
>
> *It is our embodied, relational presence, and our skill with "organized improvisation", that earn client trust, optimize outcomes, and generate return visits and heartfelt word-of-mouth referrals by those grateful clients.*

In closing, we can now complete the partial quotation from Dr. Moshe Feldenkrais that introduced Chapter 1:

> *"Movement is life, life is a process.*
> *Improve the quality of the process and you*
> *improve the quality of life itself."*

While it took us quite a few pages to say the same thing, we hope you now have a better sense of how movement, the learning process, and quality of life all go together, hand in glove. As practitioners, parents, and caregivers, this is our joint and worthy adventure through unchartered neural territory toward exciting new developmental horizons for the children we hold dear. Along the way, the work nourishes our own spirit and well-being, and earns us professional success.

Now, please stop being so serious, put a smile on your face, and go create some adventures and fun with those great kids and their amazing caregivers!

Appendix A
Daily Tips & Tools for Caregivers

As we noted at the end of Chapter 9, our clear boundaries do not require that we leave our clients stranded without resources between Lessons. We can leverage the reality-based optimism and enthusiasm of caregivers by offering "daily tips and tools" they can use to nourish the child's continuing progress on a daily basis at home. Typically, such parent "coaching" is provided in tandem with the practitioner's work with the child as (or after) it unfolds in real-time during a Lesson.

While such tips can be quite productive, they are no substitute for in-person Lessons with the child. As mentioned, we take care to remember that caregivers are not trained as we are, may not be ideally equipped to implement our suggestions, and must go through their own process of neural plasticity to shift engrained parenting habits. We therefore don't take it personally when parents don't immediately (or ever) grasp or implement our suggestions.

The following are a few generic illustrations to help you envision the kinds of "daily tips and tools" you might offer a particular client:

- A caregiver's effectiveness will always be proportional to his or her own unhurried self-awareness, which is transmitted naturally to the child through daily observations, interactions, and modeling. When a parent is stressed, the child is also likely being rushed through her daily activities; most probably there will not be the time, comprehension, or motivation for new learning. We can therefore remind and coach caregivers to breathe and slow down, attending to the quality and spaciousness of their daily routines with the child, such as dressing, eating, bathing, being carried, etc.

- More specifically, we can invite a parent to get acquainted with the movements that we want their child to experience. For example, caregivers can learn to transition to and from a lying or sitting position by gently rolling and arcing their bodies. Or, parents can experience for themselves the difference between turning or reaching when the pelvis and belly are locked and the spine is rigid, versus turning or reaching with a dynamic pelvis and spine, and a free belly. Such awareness can be incorporated into routine movements at home, in the car, on outings, even at work. When parents "get" the gracefulness and functionality of these fluid movements, they will automatically model them for the child. Thus, we don't ask the caregiver to "do" these movements "to" the child. Rather, we trust that the parents will "be" with the child differently and more fluidly, such that new learning will evolve organically.

- Other learning can be specifically invited and cultivated. We can educate caregivers about eliciting the child's fuller "participation" in daily activities. Instead of doing everything "for" or "to" the child – quickly and "efficiently"– parents can slow it all down and give the child opportunities for self-agency. For example, when dressing the child, the caregiver might say: "Now it's time to put your hand, and then your arm, through the sleeve". Then wait a moment to create a "gap" between the words and action. This gives the child time to register what is happening. Or, "I will now put the spoon to your lips" (and each time to different parts of the lips), and then leave a gap. And so on. In this manner, kids learn how communication and action go together, leading to better comprehension and participation. Most children, when given the space to receive and process such information, will naturally "move toward" the process and begin to experiment, such as trying to open their fist and help move their hand into the sleeve, or focusing their eyes and bringing their mouth to the food, etc. These are small yet empowering daily learning opportunities, and of course build over time.

- Similarly, parents of children with chronic spasticity can support the child's awareness and help them learn to "soften" their rigid holding patterns. For example, parents can pick a fun name like "lazy legs" or "soft arms", and ask their usually stiff-legged or rigid-armed child to participate a little more in daily activities: "Please do lazy legs now and you can help mama carry you (or to sit you down, lay you down, change your diaper, etc) – let's do this together". Or, "Please do soft arms now and give papa a nice hug". Such intimate invitations can activate the child's emotional awareness. They help even the non-verbal child notice the difference between "tighter" and "softer" limbs, their personal power in flexing and movement, and new ways to use their body. Again, this can be an incremental yet empowering learning process – for caregivers as much as for the child.

- Some parents are hesitant or even intimidated about physically connecting with the child's spasticity, or conversely with the lack of tone and "floppiness". We can encourage caregivers to instead get curious and playfully explore hands and feet with the child. Like the game "this little piggy" with toes or fingers, the parent through their gentle touch can slowly explore and move the bones and joints of the child's hands and feet, while talking with the child in a playful way. This is not only fun, but enhances the child's sensations, self-awareness, and differentiation. A resulting "softening" in held body parts is quite common. This can be done in the bath, in bed, when reading a story, at the park, or riding in a car. The child will almost certainly respond.

- The way smaller children are carried can become a major learning opportunity, particularly for kids who have severe rigidity and "straight" legs. If the child is physically capable, we can show caregivers how to have the child wrap her legs around either side of the adult's hip, which supports the child under her pelvis while still allowing the pelvis greater mobility. This in turn leads to a freer lower back and spine, and the child's ability to experiment with uprightness. One can even use a "baby hip carrier" that incorporates a seat at the height of the hip bone; the child is sitting on a seat that is in effect an extension of the adult's hip, providing more room for the child to straddle her legs with pelvic mobility, while also making life a bit easier for the caregiver.

- It can be challenging to bend a spastic child's legs when changing diapers, a time when kids can get particularly excited and tense. As before, the parent can invite greater participation: "Let's do this together, help me bend your legs so I can roll up your bottom". We can also teach parents a physiological trick: There is a spot under the ball of the foot that, when gently pressed with the thumb while turning the foot and bringing it in the direction of the child's face, will cause the leg to bend. We do this while talking to the child: "Your legs are now bending and this is great, thank you for helping me to do this!" The child comes to experience for himself this differentiation.

- Another daily opportunity for learning comes at the dining table. Whatever arrangement the parent has for the child — such as a high chair, a tray, sitting on the lap, etc. — we can show the parent how to arrange it so as to optimize the child's ability to move while eating. For example, is the eating surface at the proper height to optimize fluid movement? Is the child comfortably on his sit bones? Can he readily shift weight, rather than slump or extend with a rigid spine and pelvis? Can knees and legs bend, based on good leg support so feet can push off? Would strategic placement of soft cushions or balls into the lower back help accomplish these goals? Such attention to daily details can make a big learning difference over time.

- It might seem obvious, but a surprising number of parents dress their children in tight-fitting clothing or heavy, stiff shoes. We can gently point out that the child needs less constriction, not more, to fully explore the Experiential Movement process we are offering. Not to mention that looser clothing and lighter, softer shoes can make the caregiver's daily tasks much easier!

- Ironically, some parents are so passionate about helping their kids to "make progress" that they may go a bit "overboard" on stimulation. For example, multiple weekly therapies might overwhelm and shut down the child, rather than activate and nourish her native learning process (we can instead model a slower and more subtle approach, as illustrated by numerous client vignettes in Chapter 11). Or, an enthusiastic father might love his daughter's squeals of delight when being tossed in the air, not realizing that her habituated spasticity will be aggravated as a result (we can offer options for a more suitable yet equally enthusiastic playtime). Or, a mother may believe that a rigid, repetitive daily routine is necessary for her child, whereas strategic variations could be more likely to elicit the learning process. In each case, we can offer parents options with which they can experiment.

These examples are just a few of many possible "daily tips and tools" for parents and caregivers. What our suggestions all have in common is that the adults *slow down* and become more *self-aware*. Whether by automatic modeling or intentional invitation, adults translate and transmit their own unhurried awareness into their interactions with the child, thereby evoking and supporting the child's *native learning process*. Through these experiences caregivers learn (just like us practitioners) to let go of rigid expectations regarding the timing and specifics of behaviors and developmental "milestones". They instead develop a more fluid, flexible, and subtle view of their child's learning *process*.

All that said, this learning must be viewed realistically for what it is: Interim *support* between in-person Lessons, not a *substitute* for the practitioner's embodied, relational presence.

When a caregiver becomes ready for a fuller learning adventure, we of course encourage them to enroll in one of our experiential parent seminars, or our complete *NeuroHorizons* training program.

Appendix B
The Feeling Child

As noted in Chapter 4, "personal organization" is not solely about *how* we move. Our young clients with developmental deficits and constricted movement often lack access to certain sensations, and carry unconscious or held emotions. When a child explores new variations and differentiation, unexpected and unfamiliar feelings may arise, which the child might express in a variety of ways. Awareness, attitudes, and behaviors will all change. One of our roles as practitioners is to welcome and integrate these unpredictable waves into our "dance" with the child.

- As an initial matter, it is helpful to recall that the *interdependence* of "body, mind, and emotions" is now well accepted within the psychological and medical professions. Our personal history, held musculature, reflexive movements (or lack of free movement), and states of mind and vitality are all intertwined. Undesirable habits and behaviors may reflect early (and perhaps repressed or forgotten) injury, stress, or trauma. If not addressed, these patterns persist in the form of engrained neural networks, for years or a lifetime. One of the great satisfactions of our work with the kids is that we have the opportunity to address and shift such patterns relatively early in a child's life.

- Thus, in a Lesson with a child we may "think" that we are "simply" exploring some aspect of the body or movement — such as how the child uses her limbs, pelvis, or spine; her habitual posture or gait; or her chronic tightness around the head, face, neck, and shoulders. Yet, in the process of self-discovery all manner of pre-verbal or otherwise unconscious material associated with this "holding" — including strain, discomfort, pain, or fear — may spring into awareness. This can be an emotional as well as a liberating moment, and a number of such moments are described in the client vignettes presented in Chapter 11.

- It follows that in the course of a Lesson — when the child is attentive, open, sensitive, and thus perhaps more "vulnerable" than usual — movement sequences may at times touch into such unfamiliar places. The child will experience a rush of sensation or emotion, and exhibit uncharacteristic chatting, anxiety, crying, or laughing. All that is required of the practitioner in the *moment* is to allow the feelings to (safely) express, and thereby support the child in new awareness and differentiation.

- Hence, our first step is to welcome, rather than repress, the child's expression of such unscripted emotional material. This is an integral part of the child's neural plasticity and native learning process. Indeed, discovering her inner landscape and "vulnerability" expands the child's neural map, and is essential for both her physical and emotional growth and vitality. So we take care not to pass judgement, or make these expressions "bad", or distract or deflect, or "analyze" with some kind of "talk therapy", or otherwise shut them down (see the possible exception below).

- Depending entirely on the child and the circumstances, we may give her "space" to be alone (or with the parent) in order to work through her feelings or "meltdown"; or, we might incorporate the feelings into a relevant movement sequence or empowering action, such as pushing, self-supporting, or verbalizing the feeling or fear; or, we could offer her a more quiet experience of staying "present" and "safe" with the inner experience. In any case, we honor the child's experience and support her to use it to become more aware of herself.

- Most of the time a child's emotionality during a Lesson arises from the Lesson experience itself; it is part of the learning process. Yet, there will be times when the child's expressions and "acting out" are vestiges of old patterns, and hinder learning. How do we discern this?

  Consider that as mature adults we generally know when we are experiencing a genuinely new sensation or feeling — typically it seems unfamiliar and "fresh". Conversely, we can tell (at least upon reflection) when we are "recycling" or "looping" in old familiar stories, complaints, grudges, blame, and demands. By recognizing this distinction within ourselves, it is easier to see what is going on for our young clients, who likely have not yet learned the difference.

- If it appears that the child is reactive and recycling habituated, defensive coping strategies, this will effectively frustrate the learning process. The child may have an understandable fear of strangers (including the practitioner), or of "scary" new movement experiences. She may be unable to stay still long enough to tune in to her inner landscape and develop an empowered sense of self. She may be accustomed to whining and demanding, or perhaps have an engrained "Save me I'm helpless" attitude. A caregiver may typically do everything "to" or "for" her, so the child reacts negatively when invited to do something for herself. Whatever the source of the reactivity, as practitioners we sometimes walk a fine line: We balance our compassionate embrace of a child's emotional reality on the one hand, with how we might (non-judgmentally) use various strategies to bring the child back to herself and her ability *in this moment* to make choices and take positive action that promote the learning process. Several approaches to such circumstances are reflected in the client vignettes of Chapter 11.

- Through all such unscripted and unforeseeable emotionality, we hold in our consciousness the bigger picture: Experiential Movement Lessons help lead the child into a more intimate relationship with her inner landscape and *whole* self. The integration and organization she experiences can at first be disconcerting or uncomfortable, but ultimately will be functional, pleasurable, and empowering. In becoming more organized, it is no longer possible or useful (for either child or adult) to disregard important feelings, discomforts, or fears associated either with habituated and disorganized movements, or with the new possibilities. Our embodied, relational presence with our young clients helps them integrate their increasingly differentiated movement, choices and self-agency, and thereby both emotional and physical vitality.

Appendix C
About "Distance Learning"

We have published this *Primer* in the midst of the "Great Pause" of the 2020 virus pandemic. Many movement practitioners and their clients cannot meet in person, owing to health concerns and travel restrictions. Parents and professionals alike are hungering to make connections. Understandably, there has been a rush to experiment with long-distance "coaching", "teaching" and even "movement lessons" via video conferencing. It is important to distinguish the occasions when such "distance learning" can be of service, and when it cannot.

Parent "Coaching" From a Distance

As noted in *Appendix A*, there are a number of practical attitudes and actions parents can learn that nourish the child's continuing progress on a daily basis at home. Typically, our "coaching" of a parent is most effectively accomplished in tandem with our in-person work with their child, as (or after) a Lesson unfolds in real-time. By knowing the child, and watching how parent and child interact, we can tailor our suggestions to the client's current circumstances and needs, and highlight the relevance.

<u>What May Work</u>: In some cases we can effectively offer caregivers tips and tools from afar, particularly when we already have worked with them in person. Even with some new parents

we have never met, it may be possible to help them slow down and become more attentive to the manner, quality, and spaciousness of their daily routines with the child (such as dressing, eating, bathing, being carried, diaper changing, etc.). We can perhaps show caregivers how to use simple movement, communication, and strategic timing to invite greater participation from the child in ways that promote variation, self-agency, and learning. We might suggest playful and emotionally meaningful interactions that promote the child's self-awareness and differentiation. We can educate parents about relaxing their expectations for "outcomes", and to better appreciate the child's native learning *process*. And, we can do our best to answer basic questions (but we are necessarily limited by our lack of personal familiarity with child and parent).

Whatever benefits come from our interim tips and tools, we do not pretend to be able to effectively teach caregivers by video how to fully embody and practice our method. We instead offer in-person seminars and trainings for those who want a profound experience of the work.

What May Not Work: Not surprisingly, some parents quite enjoy the video conferencing experience. They appreciate the practitioner's observations, feedback, and support, not to mention the convenience of never leaving home. However, if this is a parent whose child has never (or rarely) been to us for in-person Lessons, the downside is apparent. As practitioners we really don't know the child or parent, beyond what we can glean from our video screen. Nor do the parents have any real clue about the context or significance of our suggestions, as they have not experienced our style of work, or their child's response to our embodied, relational presence as we "dance" with *all* of our many senses. Under such limiting circumstances, our "coaching" is necessarily cramped, and may largely miss the mark for a particular parent-child relationship.

We have also noted a natural tendency for some caregivers to believe that these convenient and insightful (yet inherently limited) video visits are what our work is all about. They come to expect the practitioner to provide new insights and instructions at each next call, and in the comfort of their own home (and familiar habits). There may be little understanding of why their child could benefit far more from in-person Lesson intensives, and in a novel environment. These of course require extra effort and expense. Before long, some caregivers want the practitioner to be "teaching" them online how to do our work. To the extent we try to oblige, even in small ways, such caregivers come to believe that the full value of our method can be obtained — even taught — via video conference.

"Lessons" From a Distance

As for offering actual Lessons to children (or parents) over video links, the possibilities are limited, and the downsides evident.

What May Work: If a child previously has been working with us and we know each other well, video sessions may help keep the connection and learning going until personal visits are again possible. Or, if the parent is also a trained movement practitioner (or is currently in training), it may be easier for that parent to effectively translate and transmit the practitioner's video instructions to the child. Video can also be useful when used between a practitioner and their professional supervisor; the supervisor can remotely watch the practitioner's in-person Lesson with a child, offering real-time guidance and support.

Beyond these specific uses, the inherent limitations of "distance lessons" are apparent, for both child and parent.

<u>What May Not Work For the Kids</u>: It is virtually impossible over a video link to generate the learning *process* we have described throughout this *Primer*. Cameras and screens are inherent barriers to our relational presence as practitioners; we find ourselves, by definition, two or three steps removed from our young clients. In effect we substitute a *disembodied* connection dominated by our intellect, our speech, and our visual sense (itself limited by the mechanics of a video conference, and the quality of equipment, camera operators, and internet connection). Our other senses are largely "offline". We are denied the essential relational feedback loops in "real time" among practitioner, client, and caregiver.

Consider the learning process underlying each of the client vignettes described in Chapter 11:

- No amount of "distance learning" would have allowed Sylvia and her colleagues to earn the trust of Jane, or enable Jess to discover his inner landscape, or unhurriedly invite Jackie to explore and begin integrating her tiny body;

- Kerstin could not have readily seen beyond the obvious — and opened the doors of transformation — through Julio's fingers, or Jojo's ears, or Jennifer's silence and stillness;

- Sylvia would not have been positioned to help Joshua open his "clam shell" musculature and reflexes; or to leverage James' kyphosis coping strategy into new awareness and mobility; or to recognize the need of an overwhelmed

Johnny for freedom from demand in order to start walking; or to patiently invite Josephine's new focus, head control, and organization for rolling; and

- Video sessions never would have allowed for Kerstin's transformational curl with a trusting Jeremy, or Sylvia's roll out the door with a joyous Jack, or Joann's excited leap into the pillows on her way to walking, or Jane's triumphant mastery of transitioning herself (ultimately walking all the way up the stairs).

What May Not Work For the Parents: Behind our cameras and screens we are removed not only from our young clients, but also from their parents. We do our best to compensate by engaging parents in an ongoing verbal and cognitive exchange; this is necessary in order to direct both the adult's and the child's movements on our behalf, and in turn to assess shifts and feedback. Yet, we still have little real information about *how* the caregiver on the other end of the video is touching or moving the child: We can talk about it, but do not know for ourselves the true character, sensitivity, intensity, precision, or outcome of the movements we are trying to direct.

This can place the untrained parent in an untenable and often stressful position as the "middleman", or a kind of "surrogate" practitioner. In effect, we are asking the caregiver to serve as a simultaneous two-way translator for both professional and child, without first having learned the two different languages we are speaking. Such challenges can be distracting and frustrating for practitioner, parent, and child alike. This is not likely conducive to creating the spacious, spontaneous, and self-empowering learning opportunities we want for the kids.

Ironically and sadly, if the parents do not see good results from this incomplete and often stressful "distance lesson" approach, they may erroneously conclude that our movement method itself (rather than the inherent limitation of video conferencing) does not work for their child. Conversely, if the parent perceives some good result, they may incorrectly conclude that a video lesson is all their child really needs; they imagine that they are able to "do it to" or "do it for" the child and "get outcomes", without in-person Lessons with the practitioner. Either way, the child's native learning process is not well served.

Remembering the Essence of Who and How We are

As much as we might like video technology to serve us and our clients, its utility is limited. By definition it creates barriers and eliminates much of our awareness, toolkit, and opportunity to *envision, elicit,* and *empower.* What can get lost in the picture (pun intended) of "distance learning" is the very essence of *who, and how, we are as practitioners and teachers,* and the unique *learning process we offer.* In effect, we risk renouncing our *marvelous métier* of embodied, relational presence — our *"professional superpower"* — exchanging it for a disembodied shadow of our work and ourselves.

Which is why both of us authors emphasize *in-person* and *highly personalized* Lessons, parent instruction, and professional trainings.

GLOSSARY
Key Terms and Concepts

(Note: These items are listed in a conceptual, not alphabetical order)

- *Experiential Movement*

The human brain and nervous system learn and organize themselves primarily through the *experience* of movement. Thus, *aware* and *intentional* movement is an everyday yet potent way to elicit profound changes in ourselves and our clients. Our attention results in new skills, options, ease, and vitality – first for ourselves, and ultimately for our clients. Gentle, directed Experiential Movement *sequences* help the nervous system integrate the whole self – how we use particular parts of our body, how those parts interrelate with each other, and how each movement ultimately involves our entire body and sense of self. We are activating our inborn neural plasticity, and creating new neural networks.

- *Neural Networks*

Our body is a collection of *neural networks* – groupings of nerve cells that "fire and wire together" and are responsible for some aspect of how we experience, perceive, interpret, react to, and move in our environment. The networks we use the most (usually via our unconscious habits) become stronger and endure – whether for good or ill. With intention and attention we can change undesirable habits, by activating our neural plasticity. Experiential Movement is a powerful tool and framework for evoking new learning and expanding our neural territory.

- *Neural Plasticity*

We are all born with the capacity for neural plasticity, through which new neural networks and "maps" can be formed and eventually displace the primacy of older patterns and habits that no longer serve. Children are particularly receptive and adaptive when it comes to creating new networks, in response to new information and stimuli (such as Experiential Movement Lessons). We often must *intend* to make these changes, or at least welcome rather than resist new information and experiences when they knock on the doors of our awareness. As practitioners, our personal and professional work is about opening those doors to new neural horizons, for ourselves and for our young clients.

- *Neural Maps Are Not the Territory*

We start our work with each child based on her existing "neural map" and developmental impasse. These comprise where the child is now, not where practitioner or parent thinks she "should" be. Yet, that habituated map is not the territory: It is our starting point, but never the ending point. Our distinction as practitioners is that we are in effect inviting each child to gently and unhurriedly "dance" with us in a joint adventure of discovery beyond the current map — and in fact to grow and expand the child's neural territory — through intentional movement Lessons that elicit the child's native learning process.

- *Native Learning*

As practitioners we are not trying to "*fix*" or "*manage*" a child's developmental challenge or disability. We do not attempt to "*do it to*" or "*do it for*" the child. Rather, with our skilled selection of Lesson elements we are *inviting* the child's brain and nervous system to discover and embrace new, empowering, and enduring ways to meet the world. Children *create for themselves* something that wasn't there before, *on their own terms and timetable*. This is an organic, unforced *process* arising from *within* the child. As practitioners we help elicit and frame this *native exercise of neural plasticity*, but we cannot impose or control it.

- *Learning as a Process, Not a Product*

Our value to our clients is that we are a *source* of new experiences of movement, sensation, and awareness that evoke the child's native learning. We are offering a *process*, not a *product* or promised *outcomes*. When we leave any of our own rigid preconceptions, expectations, and agendas at the door, the child's learning can *unfold on its own rich terms*, usually in ways we could never fully imagine. By tolerating a large degree of *humility*, *uncertainty*, and *surrender to the unknown*, we are able to fluidly "dance" *with* the child, helping envision and unveil their own unpredictable yet optimal path of neural plasticity. Put another way, letting go of our need for particular outcomes will optimize client outcomes.

- *Dr. Moshe Feldenkrais*

Moshe Feldenkrais, D.Sc. (1904-1984) was the polymath physicist, mechanical engineer, judo expert, and educator who originated the *Feldenkrais Method®*. He was passionate about guiding individuals to better "organize" themselves and *"move with minimum effort and maximum efficiency, not through muscular strength, but through increased consciousness of how movement works."* Through numerous books and trainings he addressed the whole being — body and brain, sensations and emotions, imagination and intention, learning and change, dignity and freedom. He was the first to bring his "subtle method of rewiring" to Special Needs Children. Today, all movement education programs of our genre are based on the insights of Dr. Feldenkrais.

- *Lessons*

Experiential Movement Lessons are gentle, directed *movement sequences* that help the nervous system become more aware of the whole self. This attention activates neural plasticity, and results in new skills, options, and ease with the tasks of daily living. We are quicker to notice and turn off our "autopilot", and reconsider reflexive habits that may no longer serve us well. We thereby become more alert, efficient, vital, and effective as we go about our life. We move and feel better, and think and act with more clarity, freedom, and potency. When we can do this for ourselves, we are then able to envision and elicit such empowering experiences for our young clients.

- *Lesson Repertoire*

Much of our inspiration comes from the groundbreaking repertoire of hundreds of *Awareness Through Movement® Lessons* and *Functional Integration® Lessons* created by Dr. Feldenkrais, which addressed the movement of virtually every part of the body, and their many inter-relationships. We refer to this body of knowledge as the *Lesson Repertoire*, and offer clients and colleagues our particular interpretation of these insights and "subtle method of rewiring". With experience, we practitioners mix and match and improvise around various elements of the Repertoire in ways that best speak to each unique child. While we certainly make use of various "techniques", we do not simply "give Lessons" to our young clients. Our success hinges on *embodiment* of the Repertoire, starting with our embrace of key attitudes and intentions.

- *Attitudes & Intentions*

A child's learning process does not arise from the mere "mechanics" of "giving" him some Lessons. We practitioners necessarily embrace a set of interdependent *attitudes* and *intentions* that bring our work to life — we *embody, envision, elicit,* and *empower*. For example, we *slow down* into awareness, presence, and learning; we enlist *variation, differentiation,* and *organization*; we cultivate *sensitivity, imagination,* and *vision*; and with *humility* and *curiosity* we surrender into the *joint* adventure with the child into the unknown. We *let go* of any rigid or particularized preconceptions, expectations, or goals regarding how the specifics of each client's development will unfold, or when. Having created this "safe container" for learning, head and heart of both practitioner and child work together as a powerful and empowering team supporting the "dance" into new neural territory — on its own rich terms.

- *Variation & Differentiation*

We elicit the child's neural plasticity and learning through our emphasis on *variation* and *differentiation*. As the source of diverse and often unfamiliar movements, we invite our clients to experience themselves and the world around them in new ways, leading to an enhanced ability to *recognize* differences, *create* differences, and freely *choose* and *transition* among those differences. To become "differentiated" in some aspect of ourself means that we are capable of freely choosing among a variety of ways of going about the same movement. For the child, such new choices mean not only new abilities, but a pleasurable sense of safety, skill, self-agency, pride, and confidence.

- *Personal Integration & Organization*

The result of variation and differentiation is an ease and enhanced function that we did not have before — a personal *integration* and *organization*. A renewed sense of choice and vitality infuses all aspects of our life. The more familiar we practitioners get with our own learning process through movement, the better we can tune in to each child's unique version of that process. Thus, it is our *own* enhanced "organization" that allows us to *envision* and *elicit* a path toward an enhanced and empowering organization for our young clients, beyond their developmental impasse.

- *Sensitivity, Imagination, Vision*

Through our own unhurried and attentive experience of the Repertoire, we practitioners *reduce* our effort, strain, and striving, and thereby *increase* our sensitivity to differences. Our own subtle self-awareness allows us to *imagine* a path toward an enhanced differentiation for a child — via tailored movement experiences and variations that may best bring his attention to the parts of himself that are out of awareness, or habitually held in limiting patterns. We are able to keep in view both where this client *is now*, and where he *might be* in each next moment with some evocative Lesson elements. We are able to see both the forest *and* the trees as we dance with the child toward each new neural network and developmental horizon.

- **Humility, Curiosity, and Surrendering to the Dance**

    In our Lessons with the kids, with humility and curiosity we keep asking: "I wonder...." We tolerate a *largely unscripted adventure through the unknown*, fluidly adapting to the child's needs and native learning process in each new moment. We don't *impose,* or try to squeeze her into some preconceived or generic therapeutic formula, protocol, or routine. Rather, we *invite* the child into learning *opportunities,* keyed to her own experience and pace of self-empowered learning. We continually send out these *invitations* to the child's *native* capacity for neural plasticity. We like to say we are asking each client to "dance", and then we are *dancing together* — fluidly, spaciously, and creatively — toward new neural networks and developmental horizons. Indeed, any effort by us to control the process likely will delay or derail the child's native experiences needed to carry her to the next developmental horizon.

- **Embodiment as the Main Event**

    When we slow down and deeply experience the elements, the gestalt, and the outcomes of a Lesson for ourselves, *change happens*. We are more *aware* of and better *organized* in our movement, moment by moment. This is the crux of our personal work, as well as the service we offer the children. By dropping deeply into a Lesson for ourselves, we experience our body and inner landscape in new ways, creating new neural networks and learning. *We change,* and thus develop a first-hand appreciation of the transformative services we offer to the kids, as well as confidence in our work. We then in effect *translate* and *transmit* these qualities of our own embodiment of the Repertoire in tailored ways that are meaningful and empowering for our young clients.

- *Embodied, Relational Presence*

    Through our own unhurried and subtle experience of the Repertoire, we practitioners become more aware, sensitive, differentiated, and empowered. Our humble curiosity *creates a spaciousness* in which we are deeply *relational* with the child. We are then connected both to ourself and to the client in each unfolding moment. This attuned sensitivity is multi-layered, comprising our physical, feeling, cognitive, and intuitive presence. Our connection empowers us to effectively identify what the child may be experiencing (or *not* experiencing). It is our *own* embodiment of the Repertoire that allows us to *envision* possibilities for offering new information and evoking new learning in the client. The neural mirroring and *mutuality* of our connection more fully engage the child in the dance. There is a continuous interplay of *feedback loops in "real time"* between child and practitioner, using *all* of our many senses.

- *Our Marvelous Métier*

    Our ability to creatively dance *with* our clients in a relational, *joint* adventure toward new neural networks is what sets our method apart from many therapeutic modalities. We sometimes say that this distinctive quality of *embodied presence* with the child — moment by unfolding moment — is our *marvelous métier*, in all senses of that word: It is at once our profession and calling card; our personal aptitude and expertise; and the outstanding quality that distinguishes our service to the kids. For a comic book metaphor, we could also call such *relational presence* our collective "professional superpower", given the remarkable shifts children can make over the course of our Lessons together.

- *Personal & Professional Boundaries*

    Our relational presence requires healthy boundaries. As practitioners we can be deeply affected by the misfortunes and hardships of our young clients and their families. At times we may start losing ourselves in the drama or overwhelm around us. If we become entangled or enmeshed in a caregiver's challenges, anxieties, and expectations, we lose ourselves and the power of our clear and creative relational presence. Attempting to "manage" or "fix" either child or caregiver problems is *not* our role, in fact hobbles our effectiveness, and is of no lasting value to the client, or to us. Keeping clear personal and professional boundaries is not just essential for optimizing our service to the kids — it is key to our health, vitality, and success.

- *Self-Care is Selfless*

    Our relational presence means we are highly receptive, empathic, and caring — which ironically make us susceptible to unhealthy enmeshment. Yet our clients rely on our clarity, objectivity, creativity, and vitality unclouded by our own stress or anxious striving. So we stay mindful and discern the difference between offering our relational presence in service to a child's learning process, versus counter-productive and stress-inducing entanglements and expectations. Prioritizing our own daily self-care, ongoing personal integration, and continuing education is an act of selflessness, and essential for effectively serving both the children and their caregivers.

- *Artful, Organized Improvisation*

    With time and experience we are truly "walking our talk", and may experience a wonderful kind of artistry in our *dance with the client's native learning process*. We intuitively, creatively, and spontaneously mix, match, and improvise particular Lesson elements, variations, and techniques with our clients. Our spacious, impromptu, yet skillfully tailored combination of movement and attitude — all arising from our embodied, relational presence — optimizes the child's learning and developmental trajectory. The outcomes can be unexpected, meaningful, and beautiful. In this sense, to *embody, envision, elicit,* and *empower* is to be engaged in an art form.

❧❧

Visit the authors

NeuroHorizons.eu

Embody. Envision. Elicit. Empower.

Sylvia and Kerstin are long-time movement education specialists supporting Children With Special Needs across Europe and the Americas. They are also expert teachers and trainers known for their emphasis on developing the practitioner's embodied, self-aware, and relational presence as the key to optimizing client outcomes and professional success. Their passions include training parents and new movement professionals, and helping current practitioners and teachers elevate their service through highly personalized, experiential continuing education programs.

SYLVIA LEINER SHORDIKE

Sylvia is the originator (in 2012) of the innovative *NeuroHorizons®* Professional Supervision Intensives, Professional Enrichment Seminars, and Parent Seminars since attended by hundreds of practitioners, parents, and caregivers around the world. She was formerly a Trainer for the Anat Baniel Method® NeuroMovement® Professional and Children's Mastery training programs in California, and a long-time Practitioner at the Anat Baniel Method Center. She graduated as a Guild Certified Feldenkrais Practitioner® in 1994, and as a Certified Anat Baniel Method® NeuroMovement® Practitioner in 2002, with Mastery Certifications for Children with Special Needs, Aging and Vitality, and High Performers in 2003. She has been in private Practice in Europe and California since 1994.

Visit Sylvia at *NeuroHorizons.world* and *NeuroHorizons.eu*

KERSTIN BALDISCHWIELER

Kerstin has been a Licensed Physical Therapist (Germany) in private practice since 1988, supporting kids and their caregivers throughout Europe. Early on, Kerstin began incorporating into her work key elements of the Lesson Repertoire and the burgeoning findings of neuroscience. She is the Founder in 2006 of the *NeuroScanBalance®* training programs in Germany, graduating skilled movement practitioners in Europe. Kerstin graduated as a Certified Anat Baniel Method® NeuroMovement® Practitioner in 2012, with Mastery Certifications for Children with Special Needs, Aging and Vitality, and High Performers.

Visit Kerstin at *NeuroScanBalance.de* and *NeuroHorizons.eu*

www.ingramcontent.com/pod-product-compliance
Lightning Source LLC
Chambersburg PA
CBHW021110080526
44587CB00010B/460